Parables from the Cross

D1532356

Parables from the Cross

Sermons for Lent and Easter with Matching Orders of Service

by Kenneth W. Rogahn
& Walter M. Schoedel

CONCORDIA

Publishing House
St. Louis

Copyright © 1982 Concordia Publishing House
3558 S. Jefferson Avenue
St. Louis, Mo. 63118

Manufactured in the United States of America

1   2   3   4   5   6   7   8   9   10 WP 90   89   88   87   86   85   84   83   82   81

Contents

Foreword

As we hear, read, mark, learn, and inwardly digest the Holy Scriptures (to paraphrase the Collect for the Word), we find our joy and amazement increasing. For our God has revealed so many good and saving truths in His Word that we can never fully explore them. Old and familiar texts are vehicles for God's message to us, as we hear and examine them anew. So it is even with the well-known "Words from the Cross" and the parables of Jesus. These "words" and parables are combined in these sermons for our Lenten worship.

The idea for this study originated with the Rev. Richard Kapfer, campus pastor at Iowa State University in Ames, Iowa. I was then given the opportunity to revise and complete the work that he began. The Rev. Walter Schoedel of Concordia Church in Kirkwood, Missouri, prepared the Orders of Worship which are included in this volume in a form adaptable to local use. He and I first presented these materials to the Pre-Lenten Pastors' Retreats sponsored by the Evangelism Department of The Lutheran Church—Missouri Synod early in 1981.

Combining parables and statements of Jesus to produce the sermons in this study has led to new understandings and perceptions for me, and suggests that "ears to hear" are still needed today, especially when we deal with texts we (think we) already know. I pray that the reader and the listener will appreciate even more the unity and grace of God's salvation in Jesus Christ which have confronted and gladdened me as I worked on the texts.

—Kenneth W. Rogahn

Lent—Easter
Sermons

Repent, Believe/Respond, Act

Text: Matthew 4:17

It is traditional during the Lenten season for God's people to consider again the words that Jesus spoke during His passion. Not infrequently, we have heard sermons, especially on Good Friday, based on "The Seven Last Words of Jesus," the statements made during His crucifixion. As we hear these words and examine their meaning, we learn to know and appreciate the marvelous act of salvation which Christ accomplished for us at the cross.

Jesus' Words from the Cross Echo His Parables

But what Jesus said in His dying hours is not unlike the message He had been sharing with people all during His ministry. Again and again, for example, Jesus had told people of God and His relationship to them. His acts of kindness and compassion had demonstrated frequently what kind of God we have. In His teaching and preaching, and especially in His parables, Jesus had set forth the truth about God and His workings among men. The message was clear all along.

What He did in His ministry, as in His death, was already determined when His work began. Indeed, Scripture declares that before the foundation of the world God had planned for Jesus to come to earth and to do His saving work. From the start of His earthly life, we are given clear indications of what kind of person He was and what He was going to do. So let us consider now, not the "last words of Jesus," but the first words He spoke in ministry. The *first* words He spoke, as recorded in each of the four gospels, will help us now, as we begin the Lenten season, to prepare ourselves for a hearty celebration of the climax and purpose of His life and death and His glorious resurrection on the third day.

As we consider Jesus' style of life and ministry, leading up to and including His final words and actions, we will be better able to adopt and live a style of ministry and existence patterned like His. As we listen to the Word of the Gospel at these Lenten services (and share in the Sacrament of Holy Communion), God's Spirit will give life to our mortal bodies and enable us to be more like Jesus. What He said and did, we will be better able to say and do. Our daily life will be patterned more and more after His. We will better fulfill our calling to represent our Lord on earth, in our daily life with one another and outside the fellowship of faith.

Jesus' First Words Prepare Us for His Last Words

Where do we start? We start at the beginning. We trace the record of Jesus' ministry back to His first words. We listen to Him.

In Matthew's Gospel, Jesus' first public words are recorded in 4:17. After the narrative of His genealogy and birth, we read of the coming of the Wise Men and the narrow escape from Herod's sword. Then John the Baptizer appears on the scene. He announces: "Repent, for the kingdom of heaven is at hand." He prepares. He baptizes. He even baptizes Jesus (against his better judgment). Jesus moves to the desert for a period of temptation and speaks to the devil in the confrontation there.

Jesus Calls for Repentance

When John was arrested, Jesus took up His message and made it His own. What did He say to the people? "Repent, for the kingdom of heaven is at hand" (Matt. 4:17). The time had come for His work to begin. "The time is fulfilled, and the kingdom of God is at hand" (Mark 1:15a). The waiting and watching are over for the people of God; now it is time to respond: "Repent, and believe in the Gospel" (Mark 1:15b).

The theme of fulfillment echoes also in the synagog at Nazareth, where Jesus read a text from Isaiah and made His first public statement: "Today this Scripture has been *fulfilled* in your hearing." The time for response and action had come. The promise is about to be kept. The scroll of recorded prophecies is unrolling. Jesus goes to work. His range is broad and His reach is wide. As in the first two gospels, He knows His mission. He cannot limit Himself to one place: "I must preach the good news of the kingdom of God to the other cities also; for I was sent for this purpose" (Luke 4:43).

The public declarations are repeated in private. Jesus announces His intention to each of us. We see His plan of action. We are invited to see and to follow. The opening chapter of John's gospel identifies God's Word—made flesh, as "the lamb of God" (1:36). Jesus confronts the two disciples who wanted to follow Him. In a few words He issues His challenge—to them, and to us as well. "What do you seek?" The command follows quickly—to them and to us: "Come and see."

We Are Called Upon to Repent

Suddenly we realize how we are today involved in this piece of history which the evangelists have recorded. The conversation is not simply overheard by us. We are the audience, and Jesus is speaking to us. Like the people of that day, we have been waiting and wondering. We have heard the promises of God, always conditioned by a certain timelessness or by the delay of fulfillment until "that day." The kingdom of God, while possessing some sort of reality in our minds and hopes, has not been truly present and evident. But now, the Kingdom is at hand, in Jesus. Where He is, God is. Where He is heard, God rules. Where He acts, God acts. And He is speaking now: to us, to me.

But we have heard the words before. Can there be anything new this year, this Lent, this day, in the "old, old story of Jesus and His love"? We love the story, we love to tell it (we sing), " 'twill be my theme in glory." But can we believe it? and live by it?

These are the first words Jesus says *to us*. "Repent! Believe! The time has come! The Kingdom is near. It's (almost) here! Come and see!" Now is the right time. It is the time of fulfillment. The waiting is over. Our ears may be stopped, blocked, by the dust of time or dulled by the beatings of life, but God is ready to get started with His work of ruling and directing our lives. Jesus speaks of what He will do, and He begins to do what He has spoken of.

How can He say it? How can we say it? To pray, "Thy Kingdom Come," is one thing; to experience it happening is something more. Where is the Kingdom? What is it like? The Kingdom comes by His word, not in word only but in word and deed. He calls to people to have "ears to hear." He comes to us with His message.

Jesus' Parable Words Prepare Us for His Last Words

He speaks in parables. He tells us that "The kingdom of heaven is like . . . . " And He unwraps the treasure from its concealing package. But not so quickly, not so simply, because there is something mysterious about parables, despite their apparent familiarity. Indeed, parables in many ways convey verbally the Kingdom that was incarnate in Jesus. As one Bible scholar puts it, "Parables are the linguistic form of the incarnation." To hear a parable is in a special way to hear the voice of Jesus. The secrets of the Kingdom are revealed to special people, those "who have ears to hear."

Parables May Obscure as Well as Clarify

A simple definition of a parable is "an earthly story with a heavenly meaning." The two aspects of a parable stated here indicate why Jesus, who told the parables, is also the embodiment of the Kingdom. When He is present—in the flesh or in His Word—the Kingdom is "at hand."

The coming of Christ is "an earthly story." Of all the possible ways God might have communicated Himself to people, and as the culmination of all the "many and various ways God spoke of old to our fathers by the prophets," it pleased God to speak to us "by a Son" (Heb. 1:1 f.). God became incarnate, He came into our human flesh, to convey the saving grace by which we are redeemed. It was inevitable that He would then be in conflict with all else that was "earthly," with every power that did not derive its life "from above" (ánōthen, John 3:7). In His ministry of Kingdom-presenting, Jesus was constantly in controversy with those who resisted the work and will of God. In His parables, as in His miracles, He offered the grace of God. Those who denied God's grace resisted Him. Who would seek to kill a storyteller except those who knew they were not part of God's story? Why crucify the teller of parables while in these same parables God is set forth and man is faced with a decision for or against Him? Jesus' death is the consequence of confrontation with and by God's rule:

one must become an obedient servant or dispose of the bearer of the Kingdom invitation.

Jesus tells the story of God's desire to rule and offers the grace of His Spirit to make obedience possible. He obeys His Father and plants the kingdom on earth. As the ancient explorers planted the flag of their king and claimed new lands as their sovereign's territory, so the Christ plants His cross in the ground at Golgotha. God seeks to take possession of His earth and its inhabitants. There, where the cross stands, God marks all the world and all creation as His possession. Down into the ground the body of Christ is placed, as He dies and is removed from the cross. The Kingdom is (apparently) sealed underground as Jesus is shut up in death.

But there is also a "heavenly meaning" to this story of God's kingdom as carried by Jesus. What comes out of the mouth of Jesus in the telling of His parables is the same power and presence that came out of the ground on the third day. God will not let His kingdom be taken away from Him; He will not permit death to overcome His life. He must raise from the dead the Bearer of the Kingdom, so the Kingdom can "stretch from shore to shore, 'till moons shall wax and wane no more" (*TLH* 200).

His Plan

The Kingdom comes by word and deed, according to God's plan and promise. Jesus does and speaks God's actions in the world. From the start of His ministry, the opening words of proclamation echo His predecessor and forerunner, John the Baptizer. He commands, "Repent, for the Kingdom of heaven is at hand." He presents God's kingdom. In His parables (earthly stories with heavenly meanings) Jesus re-presents God's kingdom under the form of comparison and analogy. On the cross too, His "seven words" are the continuation and repetition of the proclamation and exposition of God's rule.

Jesus Invites Us to Share in God's Kingdom

Where does it all end? What is the point, the goal, of Jesus' ministry and saving works? The conclusion is not His death, but His life. The end of life is not an end, when death is reversed by resurrection. The point of the story is made clear when God's kingdom forms and reforms (and is reformed) in the church's preaching about this Jesus who bears the Kingdom. The goal is reached when all are brought into the life of God and overcome death through the merits of Jesus Christ.

Do *you* get the point? Do you have "ears to hear"? Is His proclamation your call in this Lenten season to enter His kingdom and move closer to the Source of life? Again His parables will be spoken, and we will link them together with His words from the cross. We will see that what He did in His ministry and what He delineated in His parables is the same saving work that He spoke of while on the cross. As we hear again His seven words from the cross, we will notice that He actually did there what He had said before. What His parables concealed may be revealed in His Word from the cross. What is obscure in His Words may be clarified by His parables, as we examine and listen intently to the Master Storyteller. By combining what He said in the face of death and in the midst of life, we will be better prepared ourselves to face life and to experience death as citizens of His kingdom.

We are called to believe His Word, wherever it is spoken. It is spoken to us. We have the same need as His original hearers. He offers us the same grace which leads to salvation. The form and the content offer help at all times. We must give our attention here. We must also trust the Word we hear. We cannot be unmoved, we dare not be untouched, simply because we have heard the words before. The more familiar they are, the more we are in danger of shutting our ears and even our hearts, as did the first hearers. The more difficult His sayings turn out to be, the greater must be our attention to His message. We must trust the Word He speaks, as a word spoken to us in our present situation in life.

Jesus Speaks to Us Now as He Spoke to Others Then

In many ways, we who now begin this journey into the Lenten season are like those first-century Israelites to whom Jesus came. The words are familiar to us as they were to them, but the way He puts them together startles us. The ideas may be well known, but the boldness with which He presents them frightens us. The experience is repeated in us. Yet it is also always the first time that our eyes and hearts—no less than our ears—are opened to Jesus' coming. He is on the way to the cross. We follow Him on the way. But He travels to His death by way of daily life and human experience. We travel with Him, or perhaps He walks with us. We are on the move to the holy places in a holy land and ultimately to that place where all holiness ends—we are on the way to death.

But He said the Word about God's kingdom, and He proves that it is true. We believe it when we really hear it from His own lips: "The kingdom of heaven is at hand." Will we go on? Do we desire to be there, with Him? Will we cling to His Word? Will we listen? Will we follow?

What else can we do? What shall we do now? The answer is given: "Repent!" Believe His gracious promises!

Midweek 2

Father, Forgive/Lost Sheep

Texts: Luke 23:34; Luke 15:4-7

The history of the world is the record of how much and how often people hurt each other. The experience of pain and sorrow is familiar to everyone. Sometimes the hurt cannot be avoided and must simply be endured. Other times the options are clear: we can resist, avoid, or overcome the pain. But when we have the opportunity, we ask why this state of affairs exists. We seek an explanation for what we experience, so that we can either deal with those who hurt us or live with the hurt. Eventually the matter becomes clearer, and our consideration of the pain others cause us leads us to a profound truth about God also: people hurt each other *out of ignorance*, but God helps people *on purpose*.

People Hurt Others out of Ignorance

Most of our hurts are caused by other people. The cynical writer observed, "Hell is other people." While we do not want to be entirely alone in life, we recognize that associating with others often increases the number of times we can be hurt. Without "them" our life would often be less painful, in all likelihood.

Seeking Their Own Advantage, People Hurt Others

It is less obvious but nevertheless just as true that most of the time, when others cause us pain, it is not intentional on their part. And even when they seem to hurt us on purpose, that is not their real goal. Our hurt is the consequence or result of their efforts to achieve some good for themselves. The person who steals from me is probably not trying first of all to separate me from my possessions. He is rather trying to get more for himself. But the good he seeks for himself causes something bad to happen to me. Very often others are not trying to put me down or make my life miserable, but their goal is to make their life better or improve their reputation. The clash between their well-being and mine is what brings pain to me.

A second step usually is involved in the process. When I resist the one who seeks to take from me, I may cause him pain. Cornering a thief and arresting him is good for me, but he is hurt. My sharp retort and decisive action to defend my reputation cause damage to the one who hurt me. And the domino effect continues. Each of us tries to do what is good "for me" without recognizing or

16

admitting what these actions do to others. Often we don't care (that much) what happens to others, or we choose to ignore the results of our own behavior. Knowing all the facts would do much to explain, even to understand, what has happened.

Perhaps that person was unconcerned about how his actions affected others. The reckless driver who runs a stop sign in his haste to reach his destination may not even have been aware of the other driver. In addition, people may fail to consider all the implications of their actions. They do what they do because it seems good to them at the moment. They aren't aware how much it may hurt other people. My unkind words for example, may seem clever and make me look good, but did I notice how cruel and hurtful they were to someone else? It's easy to be careless with the lives and feelings of others, especially ignoring what is important to them or neglecting their needs.

Pain Must Be Faced and Dealt With

We learn early in life to deal with those who hurt us. If we can, we hurt them back. If we can't do that, we dream about or imagine what we'd like to do to them. It seldom occurs to us to pray for them and to forgive them. No, it hurts too much, and we'd rather that they hurt too.

Jesus was no stranger to pain. The prophet describes Him as "a man of sorrows, and acquainted with grief." Especially in His great Passion, the ignorance, thoughtlessness, carelessness, and indifference of others—others who were seeking some good for themselves—fell upon Him. He was put with criminals. They took away His clothes and gambled for them. Some stood silently by, ignoring His pain, refusing to get involved. Some scoffed at His weakness. Others accused Him. And Jesus prayed for them. He prayed for their forgiveness.

Prayer doesn't automatically take the pain away or immediately lessen the hurt. Hurt is real, whatever the cause. No philosophical or psychological analysis of the underlying needs and goals of the one who abuses me really makes me feel better. Pain is pain. It hurts! Even God knows that.

And those who try to deal with pain and hurt in a helpful way will themselves be hurt. Jesus knows that! Despite the pain, He wants to help us. His actions are not accidental or thoughtless. God acts on purpose for our welfare. God is the ultimate Healer. He is the Great Settler of disputes. He is the One who cares for us, when we are careless.

In our stumbling and trampling through life, we are like sheep without a shepherd. Often our feet stray from the clear path, and we wander off in the wrong direction. Or we separate ourselves from others because we know that they can hurt us. We withdraw from them because getting close can lead to pain. We want to find security and comfort. We seek after "greener grass." We want what we want, because it seems good to us and good for us.

Our preoccupation with our needs and wishes ends only when we abruptly look around and find ourselves alone. Then we see where our ignorant behavior has brought us. In a most personal sense, the hurts we wanted to avoid have been

17

replaced by the greatest hurt of all, separation and isolation from the One or the ones who can help us with our suffering.

God Helps Us on Purpose

The Shepherd knows when His sheep have strayed. He notices our absence. He is aware of the distance between us and others—as great as the distance from Him. And He hurts with us. And He hurts for us.

God Knows Our Need to Overcome Our Hurtings

There is only one final way to deal with ignorant actions. The harm that others are responsible for because "they don't know what they're doing" demands compensation. The damage that has been done must be repaired. The wrongs must be made right. Someone has to pay. For example, if I'm driving my car and an oncoming driver moves across the center line into my lane, I'm the one who must make up for his negligence. I must steer my car out of danger to avoid an accident. If my child breaks a neighbor's window with his baseball, chances are I will have to fix it or pay for it. He cannot take care of the matter himself. The debts incurred by a family member will likely become my obligation, since I am the responsible member of the household.

Jesus Compensates for the Sin That Causes Us to Hurt

That kind of compensation was what Jesus was busy with, in His lifetime and especially at His cross. He who had done nothing wrong had to make the adjustments necessary to overcome the results of other's actions. When He was numbered with the criminals, He didn't demand His rights or call a lawyer to set Him free. He didn't accuse His accusers or point out how foolish, even dumb, it was for them to identify Him with lawbreakers. He didn't protest that He was being mistreated or judged improperly. He did not call down the wrath of God to punish those sinners. Instead He prayed, "Forgive them."

When others took away the few possessions He had and sorted through them before His eyes, He didn't fight to hold on to what was His. He didn't prove they belonged to Him by waving receipts and identification numbers in their faces. He didn't grab for what they had, and He didn't treat them as they were treating Him. Instead, He called on His "Father" to forgive them.

Jesus didn't struggle to drag the uninvolved bystanders into the mainstream of the big issues. He saw them standing by, and He felt the pain of their apathy, but He didn't give them a cold shoulder in response. He didn't retaliate when others called out to Him. He spoke first. He spoke for them. He prayed from His cross: "Father, forgive them."

His reply to those who mocked and insulted Him was not given in the same manner as their remarks. Jesus did not attack or abuse those who hurt Him. He purposely turned aside their anger with a soft answer: the only ultimate answer for sin, a word of forgiveness.

Jesus recognized the deeper dimensions of His suffering and the undeserved pain that He shared with all humankind. More was needed to balance the books than His personal evaluation of the situation or His desire to overlook the failings and weaknesses of others. God is the Judge of people's actions. He knows the pain we cause for others. Our harming of one another is a violation of His law too. People have to deal with God *also,* in order to be forgiven.

Jesus reaches out in prayer from the cross, as He had reached out in prayer several times during His ministry. He is praying for us and for all, when He begs for God's forgiveness. He pays the debt for us and restores us to God's favor by His offering of Himself for us. He dies in ultimate pain and separation, so that we who are far from God and one another in our words and deeds of ignorance can know the love of God.

Some people still cannot grasp or accept the overwhelming love of God in Christ. Peter stated that the Jews who had crucified Jesus "acted in ignorance, as did also your rulers" (Acts 3:17). They just didn't know any better. In seeking what they felt was their true good, they became instruments of justice. They killed the Author of life and allowed God to set straight the record of those who transgressed. Ordinary people of the world cannot see the work of God in the life and death of Jesus Christ. They cannot wisely and intelligently see the connection between their sin and His righteousness, between the pain they suffer and the pain He endures. Jesus is God's agent of reconciliation and settlement, to overcome and remove the consequences of actions done by people living in isolation. "None of the rulers of this age understood this"; Paul reminds us, "for if they had, they would not have crucified the Lord of glory" (1 Cor. 2:8).

Forgiven, We Can Help Others Who Hurt

Now we (who have added to the burden the Lord carried because of our ignorant actions toward others) have been told what God has done and is doing through Jesus Christ. Jesus sees us in our angry attempts to strike back at those who hurt us, and He intercedes for us. "Father, forgive them, for they know not what they do."

When we have removed ourselves from association with others because they have hurt us, this word requesting forgiveness addresses us. He comes looking for us who have run upstairs and closed the door behind us, because of the pain we feel and the abuses that hurt us. There is no one, neither hurter nor "hurt-ee," who does not need to hear His voice. There is no one who is too far away to hear or to be told, "I am praying for you, that our Father in heaven may forgive your trespasses, cancel your debt, overcome your sin."

When we hear Jesus' word addressed to us and know that we are forgiven, we are changed. Forgiveness is not simply forgetting or ignoring someone's wrongdoing. It is a dynamic act which establishes that person as God's child and gives power to behave as Jesus did.

Christians can testify to the effects of being forgiven. Such is found in a powerful passage from Corrie Ten Boom's book *The Hiding Place* in which, years after the second World War, she met and recognized a Nazi guard at the Ravenbruck concentration camp where she and her sister Betsie suffered and where Betsie had died. After her sermon, this guard came up and offered her his hand; she tried but could not in her own strength take it. "I struggled to raise my hand. I could not. I felt nothing, not the slightest spark of warmth or charity. . . . I breathed a silent prayer. Jesus, I cannot forgive him. Give me your forgiveness. As I took his hand, a most incredible thing happened. From my shoulder and through my hand, a current seemed to pass from me to him, while into my heart sprang a love for this stranger that almost overwhelmed me." A reader comments on this incident. "This woman took the business of forgiving seriously. She did not pretend reconciliation. She considered the depths of her hurts, her traumas, her fears, her wounds. She took inventory. She felt. She hurt. And she said in her speechlessness and temporary paralysis that she needed empowerment from a source not her own to do what had to be done."

We may be the speaker for God today or tomorrow, proclaiming and reclaiming in the name of Jesus. Or we may be the listener, stopped in our tracks or summoned in the middle of what we are doing by the Voice from the cross that calls to us. Explanations and enlightenment come later, but the word we hear now is a word that seeks forgiveness *for us*.

Share the Joy of Restoration

Jesus is the Shepherd who knows us by name. He looks for us in whatever place we now find ourselves. He searches us out until we are confronted by His love. He tells us again: " *You* are forgiven. Oh, yes, so are the others, so are the many, but most of all *you* are forgiven." Listen to His voice. He is talking to you: "Fred, you are forgiven. I love you, Judi. I want you back, Edna. You belong to me, Chuck. I will help you, Don. I will bless you, Shirley. Come back and join the others, Alice. You are included, Bob. You are not lost, not any more, Arlene. I am here with you. . . . "[Pause. Then make a point of "seeking out" someone who is in some way isolated from the group. Arrange for someone to be in the hallway or narthex outside the church door. Or a worshiper may be sitting by himself or herself, separate from anyone else. Use the person's name next.]

Now here is someone we are talking about who needs to be included in the group. This is God's child. Here is a friend that Jesus wants in the group. Jesus has spoken for this person's forgiveness and interceded with His Father for this person. In baptism He searched for and found this person. He sealed this person with His Spirit. He refreshed this person with His Gospel and Sacraments. He loves this person.

How do you react to all this fuss over one person? Perhaps you are genuinely happy to have this person recognized as a child of God. You rejoice and thank God that this person is part of God's fellowship and our congregation. You see this person as an example of what all of us are, what you are: someone called and forgiven by Jesus because He is so good and gracious.

But perhaps there is someone here who resents what seems to be an interruption to the sermon. Or who feels that that person doesn't deserve to be made so special. Maybe it's jealousy because someone else had something so good happen to them. "Why did pastor pick that person? Why not me?" If that is your reaction, there is only one thing to say. When people do not appreciate the greatness of God's love and the fullness of being accepted as His beloved children we must say: "Father, forgive them. They don't know what they're doing!"

And look what God keeps on doing: He comes to that person in his or her jealousy and isolation. He is reaching out with a Shepherd's care so that no one remains "out there" and away from the flock. He is inviting, He is urging, He is pleading, "Come back! I forgive you that wickedness. *You* are the one I seek. I want *you* with me. I don't care what you said. I know how you feel. I will love you. I forgive you. You are mine. Come and be glad."

Look! Listen! He is talking to YOU.

Today, in Paradise/Workers in the Vineyard
Texts: Luke 23:43; Matthew 20:1-16

This Sermon Is Not for Children

Children don't understand the problem encountered by the people in this parable. They don't appreciate the problem we adults have in accepting the truth of it. You have to be older than a child to recognize the inequity and basic unfairness exhibited by the landowner: he paid out the day's wages in the same amount to all, whether they had worked all day or only a little while.

We Demand and Expect Life to Be Fair

It is only as we leave childhood and grow to adulthood that we come to feel dissatisfied with other people getting more than we do, or experience unhappiness when someone else gets something that in our opinion they don't deserve. We all feel some bitterness when we consider what we don't have. We can each make a long list of things we'd like to call our own or have as our possessions. But we learn to adjust to that situation. We learn, "You can't have everything you want, just because you want it." And in the process of growing up we accept the fact that some things will never be ours. But what really irritates us, more than what *we* don't get, is what *other* people get. It is especially disturbing when others get something they don't deserve. We learn that the only way life is acceptable is when it is fair—and then God upsets the equation by grace. And that's a real problem for us!

Retribution Is the Law of Life

The law of life is basically established on the principle of retribution. The Old Testament law says, "An eye for an eye and a tooth for a tooth." That's justice. Fairness maintains the balance of life. The Bible says, and we as Christians accept it, that "as you sow, so shall you reap." There are just consequences for bad actions and for good behavior. The whole system of sacrifices in the Old Testament also was predicated on the principle of fairness. Something had to be done or offered as compensation for loss or failure to keep the law. Everything had to balance out, even with God.

Eternal judgment, in general thinking and in Biblical understanding, finally sets the record straight and "balances the books." It may be as simple as having to pay later for what was owed earlier, so that people think their eternal accounts will finally be settled beyond this life. The good will be rewarded, the bad will be punished. "Pay me now or pay me later," as a character in a TV commercial expresses it. Or in more sophisticated fashion, we may think that other factors will be involved in the final judgment, such as the death of Jesus, forgiveness, and mercy. But we still expect everything to come out even.

In His crucifixion, Jesus was placed between two criminals. One despaired of any balance or sense in the universe. He joined with the mob and their leaders in mocking Jesus. He wished for an escape from his misery, but so great was his disillusionment with life that he had no real expectation of deliverance. "Save Yourself and us," he said, but he never really believed that anyone could get him out of the present disastrous predicament. A certain grim justice was taking its toll, and it gave him no hope or encouragement.

The other thief clung desperately to the remnant of the idea of justice in the world. He couldn't explain why that person on the center cross hung with them. He didn't deserve to die this way, "He has done nothing wrong." But this much he knew: the inexorable flow of justice had finally caught up to him and the other criminal. Finally the law prevails. "Our suffering and death are a just reward for our deeds," he said. We know it must be this way. Sooner or later it all comes out even: the government, or the Power that governs the lives of all men, exacts the penalty for wrongdoing. There need be no surprise at this turn of events. Retribution is the law. We expect it to be so. We accept it.

Retribution Is Our Choice for Ourselves and Others

Retribution is our personal human preference too. What kind of world would this be if you never knew whether or not you would get what you deserved? Who would do anything if the principles were not fixed in advance? Who wants to play a game where the rules can be changed anytime? How could we live if we didn't know what was going to happen at the end? Whether the task is easy or hard, what is more important to us is that the terms be fair. We are willing to take our chances with an impartial and equitable judge or official, because we are very sure that, after all, we do deserve and will get something for our effort. We can settle for much or little, as long as everyone is treated equally, there are no favorites, and the outcome is adjusted to the conditions.

What we really fear is that the unworthy (in our estimation) might get ahead. We won't tolerate the person who pushes ahead in line or demands favored treatment. There has to be a reason and a logic to what people get, and we are troubled when we can't find a reasonable explanation for others being preferred to us.

Our thoughts and attitude quickly turn evil when someone else gets ahead of us. We are jealous of what they have, when they haven't earned it. We envy what they get, if they don't deserve it. We are angry and hateful toward those usurpers who expect to be treated better than we are and better than they deserve to be treated. We miss no opportunity to put them in their place or to move them back to where they belong. We are so hurt by their advancement and gain (as we considered last week) that we want to hurt them, if we can.

23

But the real force of our anger is directed toward anyone who would let them get away with their unfair advantage. The loudest grumbling is against whoever is in charge, for he should not let such things happen. As the hard-working laborers grumbled (v. 11) against the householder, they renewed the sounds of discontent that were earlier sent up by their Israelite ancestors in the wilderness. In their desert wanderings, God's people grumbled against Him because he was not treating them fairly. We recognize that God was justified in excluding these grumblers and malcontents from the Promised Land (Num. 14:27). But on another earlier occasion, God had given them food when they grumbled about their diet (Ex. 16:7), so why shouldn't they have felt justified in sounding out their displeasure? At heart, God is responsible for our grumbling (we would rationalize) because He seems to act capriciously and outside His own established rules. In New Testament times, Jews grumbled because Jesus acted the same way as God (Luke 5:30), because He claimed more for Himself than they thought He was entitled to (John 6:41-48, "I am the Bread from heaven"), and even the disciples echoed those sounds of discontent with Him (v. 61). Who wouldn't be angered at such illogical statements and precedent-shattering claims?

God Upsets Our Equation by His Grace

At the bottom of it all, then, God is responsible for man's grumbling. He causes it because He does not play according to the rules. We would say He ought to conduct Himself in ways we have come to expect from everyone else in life. And He insists on being the exception which proves (that is, tests) the rule. Our sin is that we think like humans and expect God to conform to our thinking. His grace is that He thinks like God, and can even convince us that He is right in His thinking and actions.

God Pours Out His Grace and Is Not Fair

You see, God insists on being "prodigal." Most of us know that word from the parable of "The Prodigal Son," but few of us can define "prodigal" in positive and helpful terms. True, the selfish son was "prodigal" in that he took his inheritance and wasted it, lavishing and dispensing what he had in a careless fashion. But his father too was "prodigal" at the son's homecoming, for he poured out his love and gave tokens of attention in an unlimited and imprudent manner. So God pours out His love upon all sinners. He welcomes them back to His family and fellowship in a dramatically "unfair" way. He accepts them when they are unacceptable (to us). He cares so much for those who do not deserve His love that He shares His tender mercy in overwhelming generosity with everyone.

The penitent thief who cried out, "Jesus, remember me . . . " came with no expectation of a carefully calculated compensation for a good life well spent. It was his need that determined the size of his gift, not his effort that guaranteed payment. He reached out in desperation, with who knows how much knowledge or conviction, to that Man in the middle who somehow silently succeeded in evoking a confidence that He was able to help people in need and even desperation.

24

The cross of Jesus Christ puts an end to all talk of receiving what you deserve, the idea that "you get what you pay for." That pattern was broken when Jesus took upon Himself the cross that He did not deserve and freely paid for all the sins of all people. He was the one pure and unexpected sacrifice which puts an end to the feeling that God does not treat us fairly. God gives His Son into death, contrary to all that is just and right (for Jesus had not "earned" death and did not deserve to die). Jesus takes the place of sinners who deserve to die and bears their guilt. He takes the place of the God who deserves honor and glory instead of grumbling and dissatisfaction.

God Insists on Being Gracious to All

God's joy is to save the least deserving. Paul knew himself to be the "chief of sinners," but God redeemed him from destruction and made him an apostle to proclaim God's good news. He was changed from a model worker, who could lay claim to just payment for hard and diligent service rendered, into an apostle who worked because it was the grace of God that worked in him. Jesus in His ministry reached out to all, but in His tender mercy He welcomed open sinners and those whose wicked lives offended the "righteous" who were zealously serving God. In the terms of the parable in Matthew 20, God even flaunts His grace by "setting up" those who worked long and hard. He delays payment to them until last. He seems to tease these diligent laborers and even to delude them into thinking they had earned a greater recompense than had been earlier agreed to. He impresses everyone with His lavish generosity.

Those who worked all day long would have been satisifed with the promised wages—if only the others hadn't already been "overpaid." And we can be happy with the hope of heaven until someone suggests that even a mass murderer like Adolf Hitler could inherit heaven by grace if he accepted the forgiveness and reconciliation which Jesus offers and conveys to all. That doesn't seem fair, we grumble. Nor are we happy with a "deathbed conversion" such as the thief experienced. We must recall that God need not justify His loving actions or explain why He is so good, for He is almighty and autonomous. He *can* do what He wants with what He has. Everything belongs to Him. And because He is so loving, it is beyond our expectation of right and wrong when he shows how He *wants to* deal with us—or with others. He is above the law of justice. He is a God of LOVE.

There is no rational explanation of why God deals with latecomers and desperate seekers of His mercy with such kindness. There is no human justification for Jesus to share His kingdom with criminals. There is no reason we can determine why even the despisers and grumblers are given the promise. The only answer, and it is beyond our comprehension, is that God's grace and Christ's love are so great that they defy our efforts to understand them. And we dare not limit them by our own smallness of heart or bitter spirit of envy.

Children Expect to Get the Undeserved Gift

Jesus knew the Father in heaven as a caring God. As the only Son of the

Father it is His nature to share what He was given by the Father. Jesus looks ahead, beyond the cross, with confidence and conviction about the Paradise He will enter after His death. He promises, "Today you will be with Me in Paradise." It is Paradise to be with Christ. It is Paradise to be welcomed by the Father, to be ushered into His presence at the side of the One who is beside each of us in our life and in our death, and who will never abandon us to the terrors of a justice and retribution that condemns us.

Children cannot appreciate our adult displeasure at others getting something for nothing. Children expect to receive undeserved gifts. The children of God can learn from them: expect undeserved mercy and forgiveness from God, and in Christ you will get it. Perhaps already TODAY.

Midweek 4

Son . . . Mother/The Good Samaritan

Texts: John 19:26-27; Luke 10:29-37

Good Samaritans Are in Great Demand But Short Supply

Everybody *needs* "a Good Samaritan." We all have pains and sorrows, distresses and troubles, that lead us to seek help from someone else beyond ourselves. We recognize that we cannot deal with all the problems of life from our own resources. Anxiously we look elsewhere and wait desperately for someone to come to our aid. Everybody *wants* "a Good Samaritan," someone who helps just because we need help and not because the help is part of an expected arrangement or agreed-upon exchange. We are accustomed to exchanging services with family or friends, but we need someone more gracious too. We have been set upon, physically, emotionally, mentally, spiritually, and we lie helpless. And we have only a faint expectation that anyone cares about us or wants to help. People don't usually help just to be helpful, but we wish someone cared enough to rescue or relieve us when we are in need.

Everybody needs a Good Samaritan and everybody wants a Good Samaritan, but nobody wants to *be* a Good Samaritan to others. Good Samaritans are like purple cows, as in the little poem:

"I never saw a purple cow,
I never hope to see one,
But I can tell you this, my friend:
I'd rather see than be one."

Everybody hurts, but who will help? Who will think about others? Who will go beyond just talk about the needs of others? Who will DO what is necessary to relieve the pains and suffering of others? Even the best of us, when confronted by poverty, hunger, homelessness, distress of any kind, seldom go beyond forming a committee or setting up a study group or just telling someone "Ain't it awful?" Good Samaritans can only be created by God, who uses Jesus to be a Good Samaritan to us.

Some People Cannot Be Concerned with Others

We Are Concerned with Ourselves

Some people don't even *think* about the pains of others. They are so

27

self-centered that they think that the world revolves around them. In fact, we all think that way. I am at the center of the universe, when it comes to providing help or even being interested. Some people have such pain themselves that they cannot give effort to thinking about someone else. We may be hurting so badly that our view cannot extend beyond our own pain. When I have a headache, I hurt too much to think about what you might need. If I am lying on a bed of pain, I pray and think about relief for myself. I cannot easily reach out to you. Our natural human condition is one which is blind to the needs of others unless perhaps some natural ties force us to pay attention. Even then it may be hardest to help those who are closest to us. When common compassion arises, it is difficult in a world so filled with suffering really to pay attention to an individual in need. There are so many who demand help. I have given up the struggle of trying to rescue anyone else, since there is too much to consider and I am only one person against the world. So I harden myself against the world's ill. I learn to adjust and to accept what is, including the sufferings of others. I cannot get involved. I choose not to think about others.

We Are Improperly Concerned with God

Jesus' story introduces two characters who are only slightly better than people who don't think about the pains of others. They are religious people, intent on serving God and passing through life toward the divine. They see the one who suffers, the beaten traveler lying in the road, but "pass by on the other side." Sometimes we in the church are so afraid of being distracted from the religious aspects of life that we choose not to get involved with earthly sorrows. Some years ago we were inoculated against a "social Gospel" that seemed to be interested solely in temporally rescuing the poor, the lonely, the oppressed, the hungry, and others lacking in this world's substance. We are concerned for "pure religion" apart from the needs of our fellow man. In these days of revolution and struggles for liberation, we avoid entanglement in the affairs of men and their consequences. We seek to save souls and do not pay attention to bodies. Real people in real need are important only with respect to their eternal salvation. Our goal is eternal redemption and not temporal relief. We pass them by, often for good cause.

We recognize too the ease with which we can put a distance between ourselves and others. There are reasons to move on. We may fear exposure to danger ourselves. "Someone ought to do something," we say, in the face of mounting crime statistics and increasing numbers of victims, but the cost is too great for us. We dare not stop and care. The Chinese have a saying that dictates that if I save another man's life I am responsible for his well-being from then on. And that will be too much trouble, it will require more helping than I am willing to do.

Some People Only Talk About the Needs of Others

We may talk about suffering in the world—or in our own community—but it is another matter to do something about it. We know (like the lawyer) that the law of God demands that we love our neighbor as ourselves, but we just can't *do* it. Or we don't do it." Let someone else take care of them. I have more important things to do." [See note at end.]

Someone has to go beyond talking. And we know it. That's why we yearn for and hope to find near us the Good Samaritan who binds up the wounds, provides care, and promises to keep on taking care. But he's only a fictional character in a parable. We can still settle for just talking about him.

Someone Has to Do Something to Relieve Suffering

Jesus Did

There is Someone who comes to relieve the pains and needs of others. It is Jesus. He spent a lifetime seeking out and helping others in need. He reached out to the sick and suffering and made them well again. In His ministry He healed and preached the good news of the Kingdom, a kingdom where people care for each other. He sought out strangers, and He answered their cries for help. He acted while others passed by or only talked about how to help. When others turned to Him for help, He did not turn away.

After a lifetime of helping, Jesus was still active, right to the end. He spent a death-time helping others too. He showed kindness to strangers, like the thief on the cross next to Him. And He gave the same love to His mother, who stood at the foot of the cross. He had great things to do there that day. He was busy with God's work, working out the salvation of the entire world. He was busy to His last breath with forgiveness and eternal redemption.

But He was not too busy to care for the needy. He was not unmindful of their suffering, despite the suffering He was Himself experiencing. He was concerned for His family, especially His mother, whom He looked upon with tenderness and compassion. He reached out to His disciples, separated from Him by fear and now huddling together for security. He gave Himself as the bond between all of us, and He gave us each other as agents to help one another. By His cross He united us with one another in "one holy family" of God.

He looked down from His cross and saw not only His flesh-and-blood mother, but all of those who would do the will of His Father in heaven. "These are My mother and father and sister and brother," He said. He established a fellowship between people that ties us together beyond the bonds of natural affection. He made us sons and daughters of God, and brothers and sisters to Him.

We See Others in Need

We who have been baptized into the death of Jesus Christ have risen with Him to new life. We belong to each other now. Now and forever! We sing:

> Blest be the tie that binds
> Our hearts in Christian love.
> The fellowship of kindred minds
> Is like to that above.

We share our mutual woes,
Our mutual burdens bear,
And often for each other flows
A sympathizing tear.

But He wipes the tears from our eyes. He opens our eyes to see the needs of others. We are not blind to pain in those around us, those in the fellowship of faith. God's Spirit gives us a revelation and creates new sight, to see where we can help: the brother who mourns the passing of a loved one; the sister who is alone and lonely; the child whose parents have mistreated her; the friend in the pew who agonizes over the sickness in his body; the fellow-worshiper who has lost his job; the older saint who has no one to talk to; the fellow communicant whose body reveals to us the need for more food or clothing; the sick saints who struggle through life. We see them with the compassionate gaze of Jesus, who looks toward us in our need and is present with us. By His grace we may even see His image in their suffering. Mother Teresa of Calcutta has earned a saintly reputation by the care she and her workers give to the destitute and dying. Her motivation, she says, is to see her Lord's face in the faces of those perishing in this world. To believe that Christ is there, in them, is to receive the power to do good to them. His Spirit makes that happen.

We Do Something to Help Others

We do not just talk about relief. We offer our help, and God helps through us. How do you spell relief? I spell it J-E-S-U-S, in whose name both strangers and family are united with me. It is not enough to have the right answers about suffering, even the right answers from Scripture. Our neighbor, that is, everyone who needs help from me, is not filled and satisfied by my words. The one who lies beaten and near death requires that I provide from my sustenance whatever he lacks. Jesus' story speaks in tangible and material terms about pesonal help. His Word from the cross deals with the real needs of real people. Mother and son adopt one another, by the command and promise of Him who is Mary's Son and her Lord.

The lawyer tried to cross-examine Jesus to determine whether He could supply the right answer. He became defensive when Jesus responded (in an orthodox way) by defining "neighbor" as the one who needs "orthopraxy," that is, right actions. Jesus later gave His own "cross-examination" to His mother and the disciple, and decided that what they needed now was each other. By His authority and in His love, He gave them to each other. And today He gives us to each other, so we can be a help, a good Samaritan, to one another.

On the great Day of Judgment, according to the words of Jesus in Matthew 25, those on His right hand will be commended for seeing Jesus in the needy near them. Those who are lost could not see Jesus, could not minister to Him in the sick, the hungry, the prisoners, the naked, because they had not seen Him by faith in this world.

See Who Is in Need Here and Do Some Helping

Mary's view of Jesus was also changed by the cross. In His word He removes Himself from the fleshly ties that join son to mother, and He unites her with the beloved disciple who also acknowledges Him as Lord. The cross changes our sight also. We can see the people who are in this church with us today. We recognize who these people are who join with us to confess Jesus as Lord. Look around you. Jesus is still speaking. They are in need of love. Look: Here is your mother . . . your son . . . your father . . . your brother . . . your sister . . your daughter . . . in Christ. Behold them! Think of them! Above all, DO for them!

Some people didn't notice what happened to me just a few minutes ago. They were too busy singing a hymn to God or taking care of other worship business. How many of you saw my accident? Raise your hands. Why didn't anyone come forward to help me? You probably had a good reason. Maybe you thought someone else would help. "That's the usher's or elder's job." Or you couldn't really do anything to help, because of your health or other problems. Maybe you didn't want to get involved. Or you were so shocked that you were unable to move. Maybe you even suspected it was a trick.

There are often good reasons for not rushing to help someone else who appears to be in need. But there is more often simply an apathy or unconcern on our part that makes us, too, "pass by on the other side."

Note: A striking sermon illustration can be included, if the preacher is so disposed, by one of the following actions prior to the sermon: trip and fall on a step in the chancel, or drop book or papers "accidently" out of the pulpit. Notice now many people see the problem (most of whom will later state that they "wanted to" help or "almost" did something), but chances are that no one will actually come forward to help you. Then insert a paragraph to this effect.

Midweek 5

I Thirst/The Rich Man and Lazarus

Texts: John 19:28; Luke 17:19-31

Who Is Fooling Whom? Who Is Really Foolish?

You are all going to Hell! Do you believe that? Would you argue with it? Do you doubt it? Did the statement surprise you?

How about this sentence? You are all going to heaven! Is that true? Can you agree with that idea? Why do you disagree? How do you know? We know from God's clear word in Scripture that we are saved by grace alone, through faith in Jesus Christ. And we acknowledge that in this life our eternal fate is determined. At death, the judgment is already made—we go to heaven or to hell, and there is a distance between them that cannot be overlooked or overcome later. Our eternal fate is already settled, and no changes or adjustments can be made, then, after death.

But the option is still open in this life, so that we can reach heaven and avoid hell. Threats and warnings will not effect this change despite what you may hear about "fire and brimstone" sermons. Only God can do it. We cannot rely on our own judgment about others, of course. Nor does the condition of a person's life now infallibly indicate where he will end up. In the parable Jesus told, which man appeared blessed *in this life?* Who seemed to be prospering and well-off, the rich man who was filled? Or the poor man who hungered and thirsted? Jesus' Word from the cross will supply the answer and help us to understand the drastic reversal of conditions in this life and the next, conditions which the parable presupposes.

The Rich Man Who Was Filled Was Also Foolish
In This Life He Was Comfortable

The rich man in Jesus' parable reflects the condition of man as he stands alone in this life. However the man might have acquired his wealth, now it belonged to him. And so he used it for his own pleasure. He enjoyed himself and lived "the good life." All possible luxuries were at his disposal. He could afford anything he wanted. Whatever gave him satisfaction could be purchased. He could eat it, drink it, wear it, use it, without the fear that he would not have enough. That's what it means to be rich. His life was extremely comfortable, but such a life-style is also dangerous. Another rich man Jesus spoke of elsewhere also prospered, so that his barns could not hold all that his fields produced. He too had more than enough. He did not have to deny himself anything. Complete satisfaction was his—until the night when his soul was required. Then he had nothing to enjoy, nothing to rely on. "You can't take it with you," they say. He didn't. No one does. But there is great pleasure in spending and enjoying what you possess now.

Before that moment of death, he enjoyed himself. The poor and suffering in the world, even the one beggar right outside his door, could be ignored. The rich man's money insulated him from the agony of loss and deprivation. The rich man (according to the parable) did not mistreat the poor: he didn't even know they existed. Perhaps he could not imagine or did not care to think about a side of life where someone had less than all the things that he enjoyed. In this life he had everything. With so much at hand, it's hard to put oneself in the place of the "loser."

That's a familiar picture to us. Perhaps it's the image we see reflected in our mirror daily. Not that any of us believes he is rich. We are none of us wealthy. The cost-of-living and constant inflation prevent us from imagining that we have prosperity and security beyond any danger of loss. Indeed, we are unnerved by threats to our Social Security payments or the daily fluctuations of the stock market. But we are doing all right, most of us. Especially in comparison to others, those poor who lie near our door or are viewed in other countries on the TV set inside our door. We may not actually have everything we want, but most others in the world would settle for what any of us has. Elsewhere people would fight to divide what we call our own. Our conspicuous consumption is often an insult to the deprived elsewhere. But we can't see or hear them.

The rich still ignore the poor. We can still detour around those who suffer, as did the priest and Levite in Jesus' story of the Good Samaritan. We are not compelled to watch the news reports; no one forces us to travel to that part of town where home and food are in short supply. We have more than enough diversions to take our minds off the starving and bruised and bleeding bodies that are constantly closing in on us. We too can shut our ears to the cry of despair that covers the world: "I hurt! I need! I hunger! I thirst!"

In the Life to Come He Recognizes How Foolish He Has Been

But then comes the reckoning; the rich man dies. All his wealth is left behind. The agony begins. The hopelessness and helplessness of total loss replace contentment with possessions. It is to the rich man's credit, at any rate, that finally in hell he developed a deep concern for others. Never mind that it is too late now. Forget that it is only for his brothers that he feels concern. Notice rather that finally he has some feeling for someone beside himself. At least, at last, he looks beyond his stomach and wallet and storehouse to see the danger that someone still faces.

Jesus has said it, and too late the rich man finds that it is true: Whoever would gain his life will lose it! In remorse and sadness, lamenting over his own lost opportunity, he realizes how essential it is for everyone to escape this hell of

33

suffering and separation. Now he knows the pain of not having one drop of water to satisfy his thirst. His lust for life, his grab for "gusto," has dried into a thirst for relief, the clenching of an empty hand. He feels for his brothers and for any others who might suffer the same fate. No plan is too radical, no request too daring. Perhaps a vision, or a ghost, or a revived dead man could scare them out of the prospect of hell, and rescue them.

"No," says Abraham, "scare tactics won't do it." Especially for the rich, no warning is severe enough to distract a man from the pleasures and riches and cares of this life. When one concentrates all his attention on life now, there is no concern for the life to come. Or for the death to come, and the hell to come that follows. There is a time when it is finally too late. Too late to act. Too late to turn back. Too late to escape. Too late for anything. Too late for everything.

What a fool! The man who (thought he) had everything ends up with nothing. In hell there is no hope. In hell no one is rich. No one can buy or beg his way out.

The Poor Man Who Thirsts Is No Fool
Now He Thirsts, and Jesus Thirsts Too

What about the other man? The beggar who was destitute in this life? He is the poor man who carries the name "Lazarus," which means, "God is Help." The Scriptures speak very plainly of him, although they don't explain everything we'd like to know. Moses and the prophets testify to his fate and Jesus shares it. He suffers now in this life, and then is exalted in the life to come. He knows God's plan for His life, and He accepts God's will. He too becomes dry, but His emptiness is a voluntary offering on behalf of all who cry out for mercy.

Jesus knew, as He suffered on the cross, that the old Scriptures were being fulfilled in Him. In poverty and suffering, He obeyed His Father in heaven. He who had spoken God's blessing upon those "who hunger and thirst after righteousness" (Matt. 5:6) knew that thirst personally and internally. His concerns were beyond "house and home, wife and children, fields, cattle, and all my goods." He carried to its fullest that desire expressed in Psalm 63:1; He thirsted for God and was pleased to find satisfaction in Him. Earthly possessions were not the source of His pleasure.

Before His arrest, in the Garden of Gethsemane, Jesus had faced the alternatives: My comfort now, or the eternal comfort of others. And He made His choice. He was determined to "drink the cup" (John 18:11) which His Father prepared. He would endure suffering on the dry, barren tree of the cross, to unite man and God. The man who sought to live alone and to accumulate his treasures, receives from Jesus the true treasure of forgiveness for his selfishness. Nothing in this life can compare to the fullness of pleasure and joy that God gives in Jesus Christ. And He gives to all, rich and poor alike.

God Satisfies Those Who Thirst for Life

As a result we too have confidence and security in Christ, our treasure. We who are easily tempted to take care of ourselves first and to heap up security and comfort for ourselves are freed by Him. His presence destroys the fear that moves us to grab and to possess. His invitation to come and be filled shows the emptiness of our lives. "Everyone who thirsts, come to the water and drink. . . . Why do you spend your money for food that cannot satisfy?" (Is. 55:1-2).

In our baptism we have been washed and refreshed with that heavenly water that flows from Christ. In the Holy Supper He comes to us through bread and wine, to feed and nourish our souls for earthly and eternal life. Man cannot live by bread alone—this world's bread—but the Bread from heaven gives us His life and we are filled. With such possessions and life's real necessities given to us, we are more able to survive the apparent shortages in this life. The nourishment we receive from this living Lord gives us strength and power to reach out to others in need around us, too.

Christ is risen from the dead. He does not come to frighten us with the terrors of hell but to bless us with the food from heaven. He returns as no ghost or spook, but as the Lord of all who is also now Lord of my life. By His Spirit we are moved to share with others and to help them. Christ is risen for us and Christ is risen in us. By His grace we not only reach out personally (as the parable of the Good Samaritan and the words to mother and disciple last week) but also with the tangible and material items of this world that are needed by others.

Let Us Share with the Thirsty of the World

We cannot ignore the beggar at our gate. In a world where millions go to bed hungry every night and thousands do not awaken in the morning because they are starving, we in this country will find ways to deliver some of our goods to them. We who "have" will not wait until the next life to be concerned about the "have not's." Where those around us wallow in luxury, we will be agents of mercy to give our bread to others, to give a cup of cold water in the name of Christ.

The mouths are all around us. The cry is drumming in our ears. Christ is calling again, "I thirst." Give Him a drink. It is the will of our Father.

Why Forsaken?/Widow and Judge

Texts: Matthew 27:46, Mark 15:34; Luke 18:1-8

Speculation May Deafen Us to Jesus' Voice

For Christians, Jesus' word from the cross, "My God, My God, why have You forsaken Me?" is the hardest word to understand. While we recognize that all of His statements during His crucifixion have profound and continued meaning for the people in every age, we are especially perplexed by Jesus' call to His Father from an apparently God-forsaken and God-abandoned condition. "How can that be?" we ask. If Jesus *is* God, as we confess and teach, how can God then forsake Himself? There is no logical answer.

On the other hand, we can also come to recognize that this particular Word from the cross is the best one to hear. These words speak to our heart and situation with a direct impact. Here is a feeling we can understand and appreciate from our own experience. The overwhelming isolation and aloneness we feel in life is somehow akin to what Jesus refers to here. We know what it is like to be abandoned and without hope. We speculate about the depths to which Jesus must have fallen when He steps into the place of each of us under God's judgment.

Keep on Calling for God, Jesus Says

Children Keep Asking

But an analysis of loneliness, in Christ or in ourselves, is not the point of this message. The thrust of the Word from the cross and the parable deals rather with the question: What are we to do during the times when God seems distant? What is our reaction and our action when it seems that God has abandoned us? How do we deal with being forsaken—and how did Jesus deal with it? There is a simple answer, as even a child can tell us. In fact, children do not experience the same problem we discussed earlier; they know what to do at a time when they want something.

Consider for a moment the way children ask for things. They begin, "May I have it? May I go? May I do it?" If the answer is not a positive one, they usually move to more intensive pleading. "Please, may I? Why can't I? I really want it! Can't I? Isnt' it OK?" Another denial by the parent will not end the matter. The child persists, "Come on, Mom, can't I, please? Just this once? Say it's all right, won't you?" Strong arguments and compelling reasons for granting the request may come next, but what really wins the day is the persistent determination not to take "no" for an answer. And, more often than not, the parent gives in: "Oh, all right, go ahead. I don't care. Yes, just stop bothering me and get out of here!" And the struggle has been won—because the request was not withdrawn, and the petitioner refused to be discouraged or to give up asking.

But that's a child. What about adults? What about requests to God? What do we do when our deepest, most heartfelt requests seem denied or ignored by a God who says He loves us more than any earthly parent? What do we do? What does God want us to do? Jesus' word and parable, indeed His whole life and relationship to God, show us that we must keep on calling for God to help under any circumstances, for God is near and He is listening.

Jesus Kept Asking

The more desperate the situation, the more we need that encouragement. But there never was a more desperate situation than that of Jesus. In His dying He bore all the marks of "a loser"—just like the widow in the story. No one had to pay attention to Him, just as no one wanted to take up her cause. Jesus was mocked and rejected by those around the cross. Some jeered openly and taunted Him: "Why doesn't God deliver Him, if He is the Son of God?" Others sneered in silent contempt and stood by to see how bad things could get or how much He could take. No one helped Him in His distress. He had no other person to whom He could look for help or support.

Worst of all was Jesus' experience of the absence of God. Or was it the absence of the experience of God? At any event, Jesus was alone, totally alone, with no God. What made the experience so devastating was that Jesus had lost that presence of God and that awareness of the providential care of His Father that had sustained Him up to now. Jesus needed that support. Let others forsake Him, let crowds reject Him, let disciples desert Him, let requests overwhelm Him, still God was always there with Him. But not now! What a terrible fate, to lose God!

Asking Is Hardest When We Have Lost What We Once Possessed

What agony it is anytime to lose what was once enjoyed in such rich measure. Someone who is born poor may long to be rich, but his pain is less than the person who was rich and then lost it all. To have no friends is tragic, but to have friends and then lose them: that hurts more. It really is no better "to have loved and lost than never to have loved at all." The pain is the comparison between what was and what is, between what I had and what I now no longer have. The loss is more painful than longing for what I have never had. The unreachable I can only imagine, the lost I can lament.

All of us, as we have grown up, have lost many things that we had earlier—youth and vigor and good health, perhaps; assurance and hope; confidence for the future; good friends; love; or care. And the year-by-year adjustment we undergo is the process of learning to get along without these blessings. One by one we lose them. Soon they all seem to be gone. Ultimately only life itself remains. And then we realize that we lose that, too. First, by the death of others, such as neighbors, friends, relatives, fellow workers, or family, or spouse. They are eventually gone. We feel death approaching us. We seem to be losing everything. Death is the ultimate test of life; it is in the face of death that we really need God. At least, *He* is still always on hand. He is available. He is with us. And we call out to Him. And we reach out for Him: "My God, My God!" As in our liturgy, so in our personal experience, we cry, "Make haste to help me, O Lord. Make haste, O God, to deliver me."

But suppose that at our deaths God were not with us. Imagine how it would be if *He* were absent. Think about dying without God. Consider suffering through the last moments and hours without Him. That was the experience of Jesus on the cross. He was left without the confidence and security of God's presence. He cried out to God; He asked, as people do in death: "Why?"

Just because you ask a question doesn't mean you get an answer, of course. Jesus apparently got no response, heard no reply to His question. That proves it, for some people. There is no sense calling out to God. If He won't even answer His Son why would He listen to us? And there is the miracle and the good news: because He was silent at Jesus' cross, He can be trusted to listen to us.

Jesus Guarantees That He Is Near and Hears
He Trusted God Only, Not Feelings

The words Jesus cried are quoted from Psalm 22, a great prophetic and Messianic psalm of the Old Testament. Jesus is quoting the opening words of the psalm and the following verses detail the experience of Jesus in dramatic detail. "Why are you so far from me? Why do I get no answer? I am a worm, not a man. Those around me mock at me. I am surrounded by animals." His cry carries the sound of desperation and lostness, reflecting the work and feeling of Jesus for us. But there is more to the psalm and to the message than an acceptance of aloneness.

The psalm continues with a note of confidence after verse 22. "I will tell your name. I will praise you. You heard me when I cried. God rules." Even death then cannot break God's control over life. The continuing verses of the psalm give the key to Jesus' Word from the cross. He calls out, "Eli! Eli!" that is, "My God! My God!" It is enough, even in the face of death, to have God to call on. What counts is His utter reliability for those who reach out to Him, and Jesus guarantees that. Whatever our feelings may be, the promise of God is sure. Jesus knows and shows that God is true to His Word.

Feelings can be misleading, and Scripture never encourages us to rely on them. How did the widow feel, when the judge finally came to her aid? We don't know. But we know that He helped her. That's the point. In a following story, about the Pharisee and publican who prayed in the temple, Jesus did not consider how the two men might feel as they ended their temple worship, but He does declare that the publican was justified. That is God's verdict.

We have no indication either that Jesus felt better after His outburst. We see and hear Him as He continues to hang between heaven and earth with all the loneliness and curses and cries of a dying world heaped upon Him. And we know that this is our salvation. He connects us to God.

God Must Answer Us, for He Has Promised to Hear

God's reputation is at stake here. He has promised to hear and to help, not because we have earned the right to be heard and to be helped, but because Jesus did that for us. Just as surely as we *must* pray always and not despair, so God *must* answer and help us. As the words of Psalm 23 testify, it is "for His name's sake." It is necessary because that's the kind of loving and helping God He is in Jesus Christ. There is a divine necessity for Him to rescue us.

The most effective argument a child can make for a request from a parent is to remind mother or father, "But *you promised*!" Now it is no longer a question of who deserves what. The issue is not convenience or willingness. When one's word has been given, it must be kept or one's reputation is besmirched. Our adult experience has been so filled with disappointments and broken promises from others that we may transfer our scepticism also to God. Age expects fewer promises to be kept. We learn to adjust. We become realistic. We give up hoping. We stop asking. We're convinced that even God cannot be counted on anymore. We think He's not listening.

Children won't quit. Widows must importune. The abandoned Son must call out. He knows, and we know through Him that "one ear is open and will hear our prayer." In the face of death and in the midst of life we must abandon that acquired wisdom of the world that has resulted from too many disappointments, too much uncertainty, too few answers from those we asked for help. Listen instead to this voice from the cross, crying out to God even when God cannot be found. See this woman in the parable, standing at the door and refusing to leave until she gets an answer. Then reach out in prayer to that righteous judge who loves to listen. Remind Him of the promise He made at Jesus' cross, and in the same Spirit as Jesus demand to be heard and answered. Whether you feel it or not, He is listening. By His grace you too are justified. An answer will be given. Help is on the way.

God's Promise in Baptism Is Always Valid

He promised! In the act of your baptism, however long ago it was, He joined you to His beloved Son, and Jesus' voice was added to yours, as you pray. He promised and He will answer! You were buried with Him and rose again to new life. He promised and He will answer, and you will be saved! His Word is never taken back. His offer cannot be retracted, for Jesus Himself stands with us. His Spirit is the down payment on our inheritance, and that Spirit prays for us with sighs and groanings as we seek a gracious God. He will hear and He must answer. He promised! We believe, "My God! My God! You have not abandoned me!"

Maundy Thursday

Finished/The Wedding Feast

Texts: John 19:30; Matthew 22:1-14

Read This Parable As an Invitation to Communion Today

Jesus' parables always sound so simple, even cute—at first. It is only with careful listening that we realize how close to home they strike. The more familiar the story is to us, the harder it is for us really to hear what Jesus is saying. Then when the meaning dawns on us, it is often with more impact than we can handle. In this way we are reminded of how foreign God's kingdom is to our way of thinking, specifically when Jesus tells us what it is like and we listen to Him. It is a daily struggle for all of us to remain faithful to our Lord and to respond to Him properly. The task seems overwhelming when we see it more clearly. Yet it is necessary for all of us to hear our Lord's voice today, for He speaks of an extremely personal and important matter.

On the Christian church calendar today is Maundy Thursday. A major emphasis in our worship and preaching falls upon the Sacrament of Holy Communion, for Maundy Thursday is the anniversary of "the night in which He was betrayed," that holy night when our Lord Jesus "took bread . . . and gave it to them and said, 'Take, eat! This is My body. . . . ' He took the cup . . . gave it to them, saying 'Drink ye all of it. This cup is the new testament in My blood. . . . This do in remembrance of Me.' "

With that historical and sacramental background, we have added meaning for the parable of the Marriage Feast. Holy Communion is also connected to the word He spoke—one word, *tetelestai,* in Greek—when He said, "It is finished." Let us consider again the message of Jesus' words and ministry, by making His parable and His word from the cross a word about Holy Communion. In each case the invitation and warning are clear: "Come to God's feast, but come on *His* terms."

Come to God's Feast

Everything Is Ready and Everyone Is Invited

The feast to which we all are invited is prepared in honor of God's Son. The preparations are made, the table is set, everything is ready. So the Lord says, "It is finished." Everything that had to be done to offer salvation has been accomplished. God has seen to all the details. Jesus has carried out all the orders God gave to mankind.

By His active obedience, Jesus obeyed His Father's will for us. He was victorious over every rebellious spirit, every power and force which would oppose and challenge God's rule. He was obedient and willing in His service to the Father. And so He has gained the victory over lawlessness. He is Lord. He has overcome all opposition to His Father.

By His passive obedience Jesus sacrificed Himself and suffered, in the place of rebellious people like us, the punishment due every sin. His death was the final step in the humiliation and self-offering that earns forgiveness for everyone. There is no more price to be paid, as there is no more penalty to endure. Everything has been done in Christ. Salvation is a reality, "It is finished." God's justice is satisfied, His plan to redeem mankind has been carried out by Christ.

Christ's saving work is over now. He can rest from His saving labors. Several verses earlier we read John's report, saying Jesus knew that "all was now finished." All the laws and requirements of God's covenant with mankind were fulfilled, and salvation is ready to be enjoyed. It is "finished," like a candle is finished when the wax is poured and set and shaped. The finished object is ready to accomplish the purpose for which it was designed and fashioned.

But People Excuse Themselves from Accepting

So it is now with God's salvation: God freely invites everyone to come and enjoy what He has prepared in Christ. It is the "wedding reception" for His Son, to which all can come to celebrate the happy day of redemption. Today, in the gracious Gospel invitation, God still calls His people to come and feast on the body and blood of Christ in Holy Communion. As in those days, so also today, many decline the invitation. God gives the invitation, but also gives us the freedom to exercise our option to decline the invitation. And people usually choose to turn it down!

There are many reasons why people pass up the free meal, the wedding feast, the Sacrament of the Altar. Excuses are given. There are other commitments to keep. Business and duty call us away. Attitudes of heart and mind are long set and cannot be adjusted. Most of the reasons people give for not coming to God's meal would sound silly if they were applied to other invitations in life. Imagine these responses:

> "I can't go to the ball game. I just went last week."
> "No, thanks. I only go to parties once a month."
> "Only Catholics go every time."
> "I'd love to come to your house, but I wouldn't want to do it so often; it wouldn't be special any more."
> "Well, I just don't think I *need* another dinner."
> "My parents and pastor always told me they only went when they felt in the right mood."

In the parable, the ultimate rejection came when some of the invited guests mistreated and abused the servants who brought the invitation. Finally they killed them. Would any of us reach that depth, just because we were urged to come to the Sacrament of the Altar? Perhaps not literally, but how unkindly is someone treated who suggests we are neglecting God's invitation today? Angry comments are often heard, such as:

"Who does he think he is, to tell me I should commune?"

"It's none of his business what I do."

"Communion is a private matter between me and God."

The simple and unpleasant truth is that God's invitation to stop our normal course of events and to enjoy what He has prepared for us is *always* an interruption to what we are doing or want to do. We have other things on our minds. Our financial or personal concerns are more important to us. We begrudge the time we feel dutybound to give to the Lord or spend in His house. How often do you look at your watch in church? We cannot afford time or effort to stay around or get into even more activities, even if it is God who invites us.

God's Judgment on the Invited: Others Replace Them

Finally the Master's patience wears thin. Paul speaks of the dire consequences also in 1 Corinthians 11: "That is why many of you are weak and ill, and some have died." Why? Because they neglected God's invitation to eat and drink the *Lord's* supper. The result of scorning God's invitation is judgment and disaster. The king in the parable sent out troops to wipe out those who were more mindful of their preferences than of His invitation.

But still the gracious Host is unsatisfied. He MUST share His gifts with others. He cannot leave what is "finished" to be wasted or thrown away. He insists on a full house (which beats the "three of a kind" who rejected His invitation!) so that what has been prepared may be enjoyed. He is not satisfied by excluding the unworthy.

By any reckoning, there is a certain desperation about His actions. "Both bad and good" are gathered into His house and set down at the table. Everyone—anyone—was indiscriminately dragged in from the streets and given a place at the feast. The rules of etiquette and social niceties have been thrown aside in the Lord's anxiety to put to good use what is finished and ready to serve. No crumbs here. No snack only. No tasteless pot of unpedigreed stew, with the dregs and leftovers dropped in. He provides a first-class, number one, meal— and only the guests are of less quality than they could have been.

What a wild party! What a frolic and festivity! How better to celebrate and enjoy Jesus, the One who shared life with all—the more undeserving the better— than in the company of the undeserving? The door is open. The smell and sounds are pouring out everywhere. The reveling and singing are audible. It is "open house" in heaven. There are no restrictions. The invitation is shouted: "Come to God's feast!"

Come on God's Terms

He Provides Everything

But—come on *God's* terms! It is God who decides who stays at the feast. He decides who are "chosen" to remain from among those who respond when they are "called" (v. 14). The gracious Host provides everything, including the terms on which we are welcome to stay. He decides who will benefit from the meal and who will receive it as a judgment. By His Son, He provides all that is needed to remain, but still no one can scorn or ignore what He has provided.

Let us consider Jesus' Word from the cross again. He said, "It is finished." And He said it with force. He did not say, "*I* am finished," i.e., "I cannot go on, I can't struggle any longer, I can't do any more." No, His word declared that the work of redemption was complete, and therefore it is also exclusive. No one dare find any other way to attempt to improve upon His work, as no one earlier could afford to bypass what is provided.

Here our Lord's definiton of "worthy" (v. 8) conflicts with ours. We are still stunned that as Host He would welcome "both bad and good" to His table. We are doubly shocked when He excludes someone who had responded to His open invitation, but failed to meet the challenge when He was closely examined. "What is going on here? Am I welcome or not?" We wonder.

Consider the same situation with regard to Holy Communion. By the promise of our Lord, everyone who communes receives His body and blood. He is truly present there, available, prepared ("finished"), and given to all. But only the faithful believe His Word and accept His benefits of forgiveness of sin, life, and salvation. What makes the difference? Not whether one *brings* something more than the other to the table, but whether one *takes* what is given there as a gift.

God Makes Us Worthy Guests

Lutherans and other Christians have traditionally been concerned about being "worthy communicants," since St. Paul (1 Cor. 11) warns about the dangers of participating "unworthily" (or, "in an unworthy manner"). Often, devout believers define worthiness in terms of proper preparation or devotional readiness. Some say, "I cannot commune because I am not at peace with my brother." Others think, "It is necessary to pray or confess my sins more before I can eat and drink here." Or (worst of all) persons may imagine that he or she must first understand or define the Sacrament properly before they can benefit from it. So they are tempted to try to add some personal worthiness to the meal, instead of simply taking.

In every case (and others like them) our mistake is in thinking that we come to Communion on *our* terms. We think that we must do something or add something to what is set before us, or it will do us no good—and will probably harm us. But everything is "finished." We add absolutely *nothing* to what God offers. We only take—and that is what it means to be worthy and well prepared.

In the *Small Catechism* Luther explains: "He is truly worthy and well prepared who has faith in these words, 'Given and shed for you.' " The parable becomes clearer when we realize that according to the custom of the day the host supplied a wedding garment for each guest. Not to wear one was to insult the host. Failure to take this clothing was an attempt to belong to or fit in on one's own terms. In our world today we might compare the situation to an isolation unit in a hospital, or a nursery for premature babies. Pastors and family members quickly learn from the medical personnel that they are allowed or encouraged to visit a patient in such circumstances, but first it is necessary for the visitor to "scrub in" with antiseptic soap, slip into a hospital isolation gown, and don plastic gloves. To bypass these items, which are freely provided by the hospital, is to violate the sanctity of the hospital room and will lead to immediate exclusion.

The Unworthy Are Excluded by God

No surprise then that God welcomes all, but does not allow "partycrashers" at His feast. We must replace the "spotted garment of the flesh and of our own righteousness" with the robe of Christ's righteousness. God circulates among the guests and checks. "Do you have a ticket? If not, you'll have to leave." Our invitation has been delivered to us by God's Spirit in our baptism. It is engraved: "Admit one free." And it is signed with the blood of Jesus Christ. So then we are welcome.

In the same way Christ sends out his free invitations to others. They too are called, gathered, enlightened, and sanctified by that same (party-) Spirit who brought us in. Together we are the fellowship of guests in the Kingdom, chosen from all on the earth to be the people of God. They are all invited, but only they are welcomed who come in the name of Christ.

Communion Is the Reception Now for the Eternal Wedding

John, the gospel writer, points out this inviting and welcoming attitude of God in his description of the death of Jesus in our text. We read that Jesus "bowed His head and gave up His spirit." This must not be understood as the ultimate concession of Jesus to the power of death. He did not collapse or slump down, as the last breath of life passed from His lips.

What John means to say is that "the main course" in God's feast is the sharing with His people of that very Spirit which empowered Jesus. Already at the cross John anticipates (in 20:22) that Jesus breathes on His disciples and gives out His Spirit. The fellowship of the Holy Spirit is comprised of people who breathe in the breath of life that Jesus breathes out. So it is true that those who are invited to the "marriage feast of the Lamb" (Rev. 19:9) are blessed by Him and enjoy His presence. The great joy we know now is because the reception and meal are served *now,* each week or month in this church, so that we can celebrate already in anticipation of the wedding in eternity. All is finished. It is ready. It is complete. It is for us to enjoy. Come to God's feast—today. Come on God's terms—each time.

Now, the sermon has been preached. "It is finished." So, how will you respond?

Into Thy Hands/Mustard Seed

Texts: Luke 23:46; Matthew 13:31-32

What Is "Good" About "Good Friday"?

The classic question for Good Friday is, of course, "Why do we call it 'good'? What can possibly be good about a day that commemorates a death—especially the death of a loved one? Even worse: a death that is not deserved, a death that is unfair and unkind. On the other hand, we must ask: Is there any other kind of death?

Death Makes Us Ask: Why Must It End This Way?

Psychologists and sociologists have detailed for us the several steps which are frequently involved in the process of adjusting to death, whether our own or someone else's. People generally react in customary patterns to death. Still we find it hard to consider death, harder still to face death. And death is almost impossible to contemplate when it involves *my* death. It takes an act of God, and faith in Jesus Christ, to accept death.

When we ask, "Why death? Why now? Why this way? Why must life end?" God answers, "Life ends so that it can be better." Good Friday provides the proof of that divine truth. Jesus' final word from the cross combined with the brief parable He told about a mustard seed will help to convince us that God carries us even through death.

We Cannot Face the Prospect of Death

People today are accustomed to avoiding the reality of death. Our society demands it. We don't even want to think about dying. As sex was the never-discussed subject in another era, so now death is not spoken of in polite circles. The first reaction to the announcement of (impending) death is frequently denial. We refuse to believe that what we are told is true. "It can't be! Not now. Not this way. NOT ME!" We all accept the fact that no one will live forever in this world, but we will not admit that someone we know and love—least of all that we ourselves—must die. And we refuse to accept the idea that death is waiting for us NOW, that death touches us.

When we cannot deny death's reality, we become angry. We fight and curse. We seek an object for our wrath. We blame the doctor, or our heredity, or others,

45

or circumstances. Not surprisingly, we blame God. "It's His fault! Why is He doing this to me? What have I done wrong? Why am I being punished?" We are so hurt and upset that we are liable to strike out in any direction. Those who are closest to us are most easily hurt. But we don't care. This shouldn't be happening. "It's not *fair*!" We complain.

The next step is often one of "bargaining" with death. We try to set up a new arrangement with family, doctors, friends, and most of all with God, which we hope will avert death from our door. "If you let me live, I will be a new man. I will be a changed person." We reach out to what we think and hope will be the terms most attractive to God: "I'll come to church every Sunday. I'll read my Bible every day. I'll stop doing wrong. I'll try harder to be a good person." We ask for unlimited time, at first for years. Eventually we bargain for days or hours, perhaps even for minutes. There must be some way, we think, that we can overcome the inevitable. It all depends on striking the right bargain with God or fate or "the grim reaper" or whoever it is that determines the time of death.

When bargaining proves to be as futile a life preserver as anger and denial, it is not unusual for depression to overcome a dying person. There is no hope. Nothing can change what is happening. "I've always been a loser. I knew this would happen. Nobody can help me now." Silence follows. We turn away from others. We refuse to share our feelings and needs with family or with our Lord. We turn in upon ourselves. We try to stop feeling, stop thinking, stop trying. The little time that remains is so pointless, so hopeless, so meaningless.

We come finally to the end of our ability to cope and to adjust. Whether these stages of dying (as described by Dr. Elisabeth Kübler-Ross) come in the sequence described or (as more often) they are intermingled with one another during the dying process, the inevitable outcome of it all is death. The final stage of life is death. Somehow a person must learn to recognize and accept death. We know that—but we don't like it. Death is hard to accept.

We Don't Want Life to End

We just don't want life to end. "Why must we die?" we ask. A good question. Why must anyone die? Why do the innocent die? Why do children have to die? Why must I die? Why must I die now? Why this way? Why? Why? Why? Why is our world and every living creature finally the victim of death? We don't want life to end, as hard as life may sometimes be for us. But we know that death's change will come. We recognize the decay that assails everything living. We despise the losses that age and sickness bring. We know that life's forces diminish as we move through life. We become weaker, sicker, more easily tired, more quickly slowed down. Scientists talk about entropy and "the second law of thermodynamics," telling us that the whole universe and everything in it is slowing down, wearing out, coming to an end. Nothing goes on forever. Everything must end.

But we nevertheless don't want life to end. We want it to continue. Death is too final, too total. We may try to tell ourselves that death is not so final, but we fear that it is. We wish we might be the exception, but we know we won't be. The

Scriptures declare that "Flesh and blood cannot inherit the kingdom," so we admit that even God says we must be changed to be suitable for eternal life. But we fear too drastic a change. In His parable, Jesus uses the example of a seed planted in the ground to model God's kingdom. The realities of burial and hiddenness are all too clear to us in terms of coffins and funerals and graves. His meaning is clear, when He talks about seeds. But this also disturbs us—to consider a personal "planting in the ground" at death.

We Try to Compromise with Death—and Life

So we prefer to cling to life as we have come to know it here. We settle for shadows and vestiges of reality instead of wanting to exchange them for God's eternal light and for our coming into His presence. We cling to what we know from the past, our memories and recollections, and pray that we will not lose them. As our mind forces us to admit that we cannot escape death or avoid it or prevent it, the rest of our being turns away from the facts and tries to pretend death is not true—not for us, not for those close to us.

When death comes to others, our comments and conversations betray our uneasiness and pretense. Listen to what people say at funeral parlors, as the body lies "in state":

"He looks so good. They did a fine job." (But he's dead.)

"She is at rest now. She had such a hard time." (Is this easier?)

"Isn't she peaceful. Doesn't she look nice?" (Except for being dead, perhaps.)

"It's better this way." (No, *anything* is better than death.)

Is death ever really better? We grudgingly accept its reality and recognize the Bible statement that "the wages of sin is death." We know we are all sinners and that death must come. But we don't want it that way. We resist death, even when we are told that we are in God's hands.

God Answers: Life Ends So It Can Be Better

Jesus Accepted Death

Christ is the exception. He not only knows about the reality of death, but He accepts it. He accepted death not because He is a sinner and experienced the inevitable judgment of death upon sin, but He accepts death *for us*. In the outline of His life in Philippians 2, we read that Jesus "did not grasp" and cling to what He possessed. He opened His hand so that He might bless others. In that same way He received into His hands whatever His heavenly Father gave Him, even when it was death. He opened Himself to the unknown and accepted what the future might bring. He did not try to escape from death in thought or deed. He did not deny its personal reality. He was not angry with His fate or His Father in heaven. He did not bargain with God by making vain promises of how He would change if He could just live a little longer. In His agony and suffering, no depression tore Him loose from the confidence that He had in His Father and in His Father's care for Him.

Don't misunderstand. Jesus loved life. No one can read the gospels without recognizing how He wanted to live. He associated with children and others in glad fellowship. He ate and drank, in ways that made some question His behavior. His *joie de vivre* was clear. He was in tune with creation. He enjoyed nature. He was at home in His Father's world. All forms of life were dear to Him, and He was glad to be alive. He loved life indeed, but He loved us MORE.

That's why He took the course that He did. He died not because it was inevitable or because it was the consequence of His sin, but because He died in place of us who deserved death. He humbled Himself even to death on a cross, for us who refuse to bear our crosses or admit our death. He gave Himself for us, so that our life and our death might be sanctified, so that we might live and die as sons and daughters of God. With His own body He filled the gap between the desire for life and the knowledge of death. For us, and for our salvation, He entered that hopeless, cursed state of death.

He said, "Into Thy hands I commend my Spirit," because He was willing to entrust His life to God. His was a *total* commitment to God. He was willing to follow through and rely on God's dependability by His action. Throughout His passion Jesus was in total control of His life. He knew what He was doing, even when it meant giving up His life for us and to us. The words of Psalm 31: 5, were originally set in a situation of deep distress. It was overcome by a profound conviction that God could deliver the suffering one. Now Jesus speaks the words in their fullest meaning as He hangs between life and death, with no hope but trust in God, no help but the Father in heaven, no resources except those given to Him from above.

Jesus Guarantees God's Life Beyond Our Death

We can admire Jesus and give Him thanks for His willing death in our place, even if we cannot readily duplicate His free acceptance of death. We need not imagine that a victorious confrontation with death will be ours only if we can copy Him by a massive effort on our part. Perhaps we cannot now speak as confidently as He did. Perhaps we never will. But it is still true that the hands of God are there to receive us when our life fails, as they received Christ Jesus. As surely as God raised Jesus from the dead, just so certainly does He bear us up in His everlasting arms as we begin the fall into death. We shall not be lost or destroyed, for Christ is with us. When He expired and breathed His last, He also inspired us with life like His. That is the grace of His spirit, commended to God, and poured out now upon all His people.

God works when nothing man does works. It is God who raises the dead, Paul confesses (2 Cor. 1:9). God produces life and growth when hope is buried and concealed. God's kingdom comes forth even from death itself, for His is the almighty and gracious power of life. All of us, even in the city, are familiar with the growing process which involves a seed planted and a crop produced. We are not surprised to learn that plants grow only after seeds are planted. It is more difficult for us to move from inanimate growth to human hopes. Anyone can plant a seed and expect a flower. But only people of faith can plant a human

48

body and await the glorious harvest of resurrection. But Jesus had already declared it: The Kingdom is like a seed that grows. Or more: The Kingdom is like a *tiny* seed that produces a *great* crop.

The New Life Beyond Death Is Better Than the Old Life

In Jesus, God is not satisfied simply to duplicate the course of natural events. Nor will He settle for haphazard or casual results in His garden. He plants His very best, which seems to be the very least, so that as Christ rises from the dust of death He, the first shoot, is the precursor of the overwhelming totality of bodies that God will bring before Him. After His resurrection, Jesus inspired His disciples to plant the Word elsewhere. His Spirit moved across lands and countries creating new life. God's people carried the good news of the Gospel to all nations, so that foreign strains were included in the harvest. As Gentiles were added to the Kingdom, the words of Jesus have been ultimately fulfilled: all kinds of birds have found refuge in the branches of God's kingdom-tree. All people are welcome, when they are drawn by the Spirit of Christ.

Look at what God can do with a spirit that is placed into His hands. He can keep it safe, certainly, but He is not one to bury it in the ground to prevent a loss. Instead God nourishes that spirit—we're talking about Jesus' spirit, inspired with the conviction of the psalmist and more—and shares it with others. He makes us like Christ. He makes us alive and conquerors over death.

He ends our old life-style, when He (daily) puts to death all our old ways of thinking and dealing with life. By the water of our baptism He nourishes the seed of the kingdom that is our true life and (daily) leads us to walk in newness of life as citizens of His kingdom. In each confession of sin, we die to the notion that we can survive without God. We put to death that "old Adam" in us that exposes us to eternal death by separating us from the source of life and growth. In the word of absolution which Christ speaks through His church, we are renewed for living, opened to the future, set to walk the path of life as God's children. In the Holy Supper, the bread and wine are taken into our mortal bodies as the ground encloses a seed. Then by the grace of God, Christ roots down in us, and His life springs up in us and sends forth shoots and branches and flowers. His Spirit and power await us each time we place ourselves into His loving hands, so that He can form and fashion us into His image. All during our life God is working from within. He is working out the steps that enable us to face death, when that day comes. He fills us with the confidence and assurance that He has overcome that last great Enemy.

Eternal Life Makes Today Good

Life is good, and God means for us to enjoy it. But on this day called Good Friday we are especially aware of Him overcoming the death that threatens us each day. He not only makes our present life better by His promise and presence, but in His goodness He convinces us that heaven and eternal life are best. That which is put into the ground here will be glorified. The sad small beginning that we see at the cemetery will develop into a joyful and overwhelming finale when

He raises us up. To be with Him, to join hands with Him forever, is to reach the goal of life itself. In heaven, life will never end. The threat of loss that we experience with everything in this life will be overcome by the gift of life without end.

This is our hope. It was for this that Jesus faced and overcame death. In this confidence we face our death—and each day of our life—and say, "Into Thy hands I commit my spirit." And we too shall live, through Christ. He shall "give me and all believers in Christ eternal life. This is most certainly true." And it is good.

Easter Day

Easter Is . . . Peace/The Sower and Seed

Texts: John 20:19; Mark 4:3-8

Jesus' First Word After the Cross Is "Peace"

If you had died and rose again, what do you think would be the first thing you would say to your friends and fellow workers, when you saw them together for the first time? Recognizing human scepticism about life after death, perhaps you'd say something personal to try to prove to them that it was really you. Or, maybe you'd just be shouting and praising God because you were alive. Maybe you'd talk with your friends about the experience of death and tell them what happened to you while you were away. What would *you* say?

What did *Jesus* say after He rose from the dead? After the "incidental" encounters with several individuals, He appeared to all the disciples gathered together, as we read in John 20. And He said to them, "Peace be with you"(v. 19). In fact, He then said it again (v. 21), after gladdening their hearts with an exhibition of His hands and side: "Peace be with you." What a divine word! What a great blessing! Jesus gives His word of peace, because peace is just what everybody needs. Notice: His words after resurrection, like the words He spoke before and during His death, are words for others. Unlike us, Jesus wants to help others rather than care for Himself.

Throughout the pages of the Old and New Testaments, the word "peace" encapsulates the blessings God gives to His people. The Hebrew word *shalom* expresses a situation of total contentment and satisfaction, with a sense of well-being and happiness that overcomes and eliminates all the negative and unpleasant aspects of life. Peace is always a gift of God rather than something that is earned. Peace is a blessing that possesses one more than one possesses it. The Greek word *eirene* appears again and again in the New Testament, in combination with other grace-loaded terms to express the complete goodness a person receives as a child of God. One author has defined peace as "the quiet calm assurance that God is with me, and that He will guide and love me always, and always invites me to rely upon Him"(E. Brown, *Living the Liturgy*). Peace is having God. And Jesus is God-for-us just as He is God-with-us. So He says to His troubled people, again and again, "Peace be with you."

Jesus' Parable Demonstrates That We Need Peace

Peace is just what we need. Peace is what people seek in life. The assurance that all of my life is under God's control and proceeding in a good and proper manner allows me to live with the security and happiness that makes life worthwhile. God goes to unbelievable (and yet, believable) lengths to prove that He is at peace with us and we can live at peace with Him. His work among us now, through Word and Sacraments, brings us peace for all aspects of our life. Jesus is our Peace, and in Him we find the peace that passes all understanding and every imagination of man.

In His earthly ministry, Jesus conveyed that certainty of God's peace in His dealings with people who did not have peace in their lives. The opening and definitive parable of His ministry (recorded in Mark 4) set the scene for all that He continued to say and do to the end—and into the new beginning. "A sower went out to sow," He said, characterizing the work which according to God's will He and His followers would do. "The sower sows the word," He explains in v. 14. The Word which is sown can be summarized simply as "Peace be with you!" It is a good and glad word for us to hear. It is just the Word that people need, for life by itself lacks peace.

We can find no peace with God or without God. We cannot live in peace with other people. We are not at peace within ourselves. We worry about our problems, our failures, and our inadequacies. We are disturbed by the actions of others. We are hurt and alone, depressed and uncertain. We conceal our real feelings and thoughts. Our hearts are divided. We are concerned about God and how He feels toward us. We know that we have disobeyed Him, even though we knew better, and we are guilty. We feel guilty. We fear disclosure. We don't want anyone to see us, not as we really are. Most of all we don't want God to come so close. We fear what He will say to us, because we know that He knows. And so we have no peace.

Satan Steals Our Peace

Jesus comes to us, and He speaks His Word of peace to us. And there is relief and joy at hearing Him say, "Peace be with you." But Satan objects: "Peace is not for you. That's not true. God doesn't mean you. You don't deserve it. Your sins are too great. You are too wicked. You're not the kind of person who receives peace from God. Wait a while. Do better. Try harder. Pray. Read your Bible. Go to church. Maybe someday you will be able to receive peace. But not now. Not the way you are now." And the peace of God is stolen from our ears and hearts, the way bare seed is snatched up from the ground by birds' beaks. And we lack peace.

Our Roots Are Too Shallow to Maintain Peace

The sower sows the seed again. Jesus speaks the Word: "Peace be with you!" We desperately grasp for that word. This time it seems real and true. We need peace. We want it. We take it. We add it to our lives like the latest coat of paint on an old wall. It covers, even if it is only on the surface. We take Christ's peace and add it to our collection of treasures, one more item of the total that gives meaning to our lives. This is a peace that is shallow, that requires no upsets

52

and does not change our lives. It is the "white sepulchre" of the Pharisee's relationship to God, which looks good on the outside but has no real peace and therefore does not convey life. Peace-on-the-surface is the "cheap grace" of Dietrich Bonhoeffer; it placates and soothes but never gets to the heart of the problem, which is the problem of the heart. Peace, which is only a pat on the head or an automatic smile, is peace that does not remain. No one can "rest in peace" in this life, without the deep excavations of the heart that lay bare the truth of a person's character. "Easy peace" is the glib and thoughtless response which says, "I'm fine" (but it's not true, deep down) when God asks, "How are you?" Peace without foundation is a growth on the surface, like seed on a dusting of soil, which quickly moves on and passes away. The casual word of peace shrivels and dries. And we still lack peace.

Other Factors in Life Crowd Out Our Peace

The sower sows the seed again. "Peace be with you," He says to us. You who weep over what you had but then lost, you whose hopes have been dashed by the passage of time and change of events: "Peace be with you!" The memory of once enjoyed pleasures, the recollection of past momentary happiness, the lingering taste of what was sampled, all these encourage us to take God's peace this time. We desperately want to have peace. We deserve to have some joy and happiness before we die. We take His peace and toss it into the pot of our life's stew, along with the other tasty ingredients and staples of life. As it mixes in, the special taste quality of peace is diluted and lost.

We want to believe that Christ's peace prevails and is dominant, but we must still worry about our children, our parents, the house, the job, school, bills, weather, relatives, spouse, property, time, schedules, promises, obligations etc. There are so many things that we must still take care of in our daily life; we have too many responsibilities to commend ourselves simply to God's peace. We are confronted by the material and financial challenges of the economy, bank accounts, savings, retirement plans, cash flow, needs, pleasures, furniture, car, travel, clothes, inflation, cost-of-living adjustments, bonus, strike, negotiations, guarantees, etc. "All that Mammon offers" does not let us enjoy a moment's peace.

We consider what things we still want: the prospects, the expectations, childhood dreams, fantasies, wishes, hopes, imaginations of what could be or should be or ought to be or we'd like to be, etc. Our eyes are so filled with the vision of what we are seeking after that our ears become deaf to the Word Jesus is saying. What is He talking about? Peace? How can I have peace when I still want and need and desire so many other things. And peace is choked, like a tender plant lost among thorns and weeds in a field. And we lack peace.

We Want to Nourish and Sustain Christ's Peace

The sower comes and sows the seed. The word of peace is spoken again. This time we resolve to receive it, to hold it, to anchor it, to protect it. We must have peace, if we are going to live. "Lord, have mercy!" That risen Lord with marked side and wounded hands says to us, "Peace be with you." Now we are ready and open to it. It is the openness of Easter. We have been preparing for this moment these 40-plus days. We have practiced and rehearsed for this day. We are surrounded by song and music of resurrection. We are dressed for the occasion. We are up early and filled with anticipation. We have done all we can to be ready. We have worked conscientiously and carefully to make it happen— this time. We have confessed our sin and been absolved. We have listened to all the readings and sermons. We remember what was said. We treasure words from the cross and thoughts from the parables in our hearts and memories. We have, at least temporarily, made peace with our desires and self-seeking and blotted out the problems that trouble us day by day. We are good ground. We await the seed. We are open to His Word. He says it now, "Peace be with you!" And then . . . I wonder: "Why don't I have that peace? Why don't I get it this time? Why didn't it work?" And we still lack peace.

What is the problem? Is it again just the empty "Peace! Peace! and there is no peace" refrain of the Old Testament? *Can* God's Word perhaps sometimes return void after all? The peace we sought is the peace we are still seeking. How do we get it? What is the answer?

God's Word Reiterates That We Have Peace

The answer is before us, rising from the open tomb: Jesus is our peace. He does not simply speak peace or deliver peace or promise peace. He is Peace. To receive Him is to have peace. There is no peace without Him. Peace is not dispensed as a prepackaged item, an extra-cost option, an independent unit. Peace is Jesus. Jesus is peace. The words are synonymous and inseparable.

Jesus Has Overcome Satan

Jesus is peace: He silences the accusations and threats of Satan and of our own hearts. When charges are pressed against us, true or not, we need only one Defense: Jesus!" Jesus is my confidence." Though I am unworthy and sin is still within me, nothing can separate me from the love of God. No one can challenge my peace. I am sure I am at peace with God, because of Jesus.

Jesus' Roots Are Planted Deep

The word of peace—Jesus—overwhelms me and clings to me, though my roots are not deep. The word of peace was made flesh for me in Jesus. Jesus is my peace. He was planted *for me* deep, deep down in the ground in death. He sank into the depths of hell, He went to the bottom of my problems and tore at the roots of my restlessness. He is my Anchor and my Root. Jesus, risen from death, the fruit of God's grace, now and forevermore alive, has gripped me. He holds me (not that I must cling more to Him) with a love stronger than the grip of death. I am planted in Him and at His cross, and He is my Peace.

Jesus Has Overcome This World

Jesus is my Peace! He brings peace to me, because He is peace for me. He has overcome this world and all that is in it—"the lust of the eyes, the lust of the flesh, the pride of life" (1 John 2). He is my desire and my wealth and my care. He cares for me so much that I will not be careless with Him, but I shall live carefree, and be careful to stay with Him. He is rich in mercy and forgiveness, with confidence and hope for me. He is my security and God's promise. He is my Priceless Treasure. Jesus, and Him only, do I desire. Having Him I have all. He is my peace! Jesus has choked the chokers in my life. He has been crowned with thorns to set me free from the barbs and scratches of the weeds that bear this world's poison. He is the weed-killer. He guarantees and preserves my growth. Jesus is my Peace. He is All to me.

Jesus Is the Seed That Produces Peace

Jesus is my Peace! It is not the soil after all that determines the crop, but the seed Himself that bears the life. Peace is planted in the ground, and the result is determined by God. I receive His life and I am able to grow. "God gives the increase." I am buried with Christ by baptism, and daily rise to new life. I am God's child, and He raises me. Jesus is my Peace. I am "a piece" of Him. My attention is directed away from myself and all that I do right or wrong. My faith is focused on Him: the Word/ the Seed, made flesh, made Life. As long as the seed is present and God is nourishing it, the Seed must grow. Receive the Seed. Heed the Word. Open the ears of your heart. Peace must come. Jesus must increase. And have Peace, having Jesus.

Christ's Peace Leads Me to Follow Him

That Peace now guides my life. The word Jesus first spoke to His disciples after His resurrection was the word, "Peace," to all. The final word that St. John records, the real "last word" of Jesus on earth, is written in 21:22, and it is a personal address: "Follow Me," He says. Discipleship is the fruit of peace day by day.

Peace continues as the very breath of my life when I follow in the Spirit of Christ and share that peace with others. Jesus sends me, as He sent the disciples the first time, to forgive the sins of others (or to retain them if need be). He leads me to share whatever gifts I have received with those in need so that peace is down-to-earth for them. He calls me to follow Him everywhere, even to death, with the knowledge that He is with me. He leads me to my brothers and sisters who are His brothers and sisters. He encourages me to call on Him constantly with prayer, because God will not and cannot abandon me. Today I know Paradise with Him, for He sets me at peace even in this present world. He satisfies me early with His mercy and so fills me with living water that my only thirst is to do His will. I am "in Christ" each day and am kept by Him. He comes to me and stays with me; He sets me free from fear and doubt; I hear Him speak to me, as St. Matthew quotes His resurrection-word, "Do not be afraid."

I am afraid, of course, the way Peter was afraid when he concentrated on the roaring waters of life instead of the guiding voice of Jesus. But He takes away my fear and gives me peace. Now my fear is a holy awe and reverence at His greatness, which He devotes to loving me. I kneel at His table and feed on His body and blood. I receive Him by faith and listen to His voice. So He is for me and to me what He was in His earthly ministry, what He taught in His parables, what He said on His cross: Jesus is my peace.

It is enough. One word is sufficient. Now I am alive, too. So are we all. In Christ, we live forever. "Peace be with you."

Votum: "And the peace of God, which passes all understanding, will keep your hearts and your minds in Christ Jesus" (Phil. 4:7).

Lent—Easter
Orders of Service

Ash Wednesday

As we gather, we spend a few moments in prayer asking the Lord to touch our hearts with His grace so that we can step into Lent feeling His pardon and peace and sensing His power and purpose for our lives.

REPENT, BELIEVE
Respond, Act

Matthew 4:17

WE CELEBRATE

Lector: Welcome! Fellow Pilgrims of the Lord. We begin our Lenten celebration as we begin all celebrations,

Pastor: In the name of the Father and of the Son and of the Holy Spirit.

People: Amen.

Lector: Come now, to relive the opening words of our Lord's ministry:

Pastor: "Turn away from your sins because the Kingdom of heaven is near."
(Matthew 4:17b TEV)

Lector: And the Words spoken by Jesus in His Sermon on the Mount:

Pastor: "And your Father, who sees what you do in private, will reward you."
(Matthew 6:6b and 18b)

All: In the cross of Christ I glory,
Towering o'er the wrecks of time.
All the light of sacred story
Gathers round its head sublime

When the woes of life o'ertake me,
Hopes deceive and fears annoy,
Never shall the cross forsake me;
Lo, it glows with peace and joy.

From *The Lutheran Hymnal,* © 1941
Concordia Publishing House
"In the Cross of Christ I Glory"
Tune: **Rathbun**

WE CONFESS

Lector: As we begin our journey into Lent, let us pause to make confession.

Pastor: It is our fault that You had to die, Lord Jesus . . . our selfishness, self-pity, and self-reliance.

People: *Ashes to ashes, dust to dust, O Lord, on Your way to death, have mercy upon us.*

Pastor: It is our fault that You had to die, Lord Jesus . . . our stupidity, stubbornness, and smuttiness.

People: *Ashes to ashes, dust to dust. O Lord, on Your way to death, have mercy upon us.*

Pastor: It is our fault that You had to die, Lord Jesus . . . our sloppiness, sluggishness, and shoddiness.

People: *Ashes to ashes, dust to dust. O Lord, on Your way to death, have mercy upon us.*

All: *A crown of thorns Thou wearest,*
My shame and scorn Thou bearest,
That I might ransomed be.
My Bondsman, ever willing,
My place with patience filling,
From sin and guilt hast made me free.

From *The Lutheran Hymnal,* © 1941
Concordia Publishing House
"Upon the Cross Extended"
Tune: **O Welt, ich muss . . .**

WE CONFESS

God Speaks

"But even now," says the Lord, "repent sincerely and return to Me with fasting and weeping and mourning. Let your broken hearts show your sorrow; tearing your clothes is not enough." Come back to the Lord your God. He is kind and full of mercy; He is patient and keeps His promise; He is always ready to forgive and not punish. Perhaps the Lord your God will change His mind and bless you with abundant crops. Then you can offer Him grain and wine. Blow the trumpet on Mount Zion; give orders for a fast and call an assembly! Gather the people together; prepare them for a sacred meeting; bring the old people; gather the children and the babies too. Even newly married couples must leave their homes and come. The priests, serving the Lord between the altar and the entrance of the Temple, must weep and pray: "Have pity on Your people, Lord. Do not let other nations despise us and mock us by saying, 'Where is your God?' " Then the Lord showed concern for His land; He had mercy on His people. He answered them: "Now I am going to give you grain and wine and olive oil, and you will be satisfied. Other nations will no longer despise you."

(Joel 2:12-19 TEV)

We Speak

      O Lord, as we examine our own hearts, help us also to examine the nature of our response as a congregation to Your call to be in mission for You in Your world.

God Speaks

      The Passion History according to
      the Gospel of Saint Matthew

      JESUS IN THE UPPER ROOM
      26:17-35

We Sing   "On My Heart Imprint Your Image"
                               Tune: **Der am Kreuz**

We Listen   The Homily

WE CONFIRM

With Our Offerings

      (As our response to God's pardon and purpose for our lives)

With Our Prayers

Pastor: Let us pray for all the people of God and for the world.

      (A Brief Silence for Individual Prayer)

Lector: We pray, O God, for Your whole church, that under the guidance of Your Spirit, it may venture forth boldly in faith during this Lenten season.

People: Lord, help us make this Lent count for our spiritual growth.

Lector: We pray for our congregation, that we may be open to the urgings of Your Spirit.

People: Lord, give us the vision to celebrate Lent, worshiping, witnessing, and working for You.

Lector: We pray for the leaders of our country, that they may work for peace and justice for all people.

People: Lord, move us to become involved in the issues and concerns that face our country.

      (Here may be offered other petitions)

Pastor: Into Your hands, Father, we commend all for whom we pray, trusting in Your mercy, through Your Son, Jesus Christ our Lord.

People: Amen.

WE COMMUNE

The Preface
The Distribution Hymn   "Jesus, I Will Ponder Now"
                                                       Tune: **Jesu Kreuz . . .**

WE CONTINUE

Lector: As God has spoken to you this day, He calls you to continue . . .

Pastor: To be truly penitent in your hearts;
To return to the Lord, your God;
To remain firm in your faith and loyal in your service.

People: As we enter the Lenten season, help us, O Lord, to make our worship an honest expression of our repentance. May this Lent be that time where we grow in grace, increase in love, and become bolder witnesses of our faith.

WE COMMIT

Lector: God now comes to You this day with His blessing.

Pastor: "Peace is what I leave with you; it is My own peace that I give you. I do not give it as the world does. Do not be worried and upset; do not be afraid."

(John 14:27 TEV)

Lector: What is your response?

People: We go forth with God's pardon, experiencing His peace, being assured of His promises, feeling His power, and seeking His purpose for our daily lives.

Pastor: Go now in peace, loving and serving the Lord, rejoicing in the forgiveness given to you through Jesus Christ.

People: Amen.

    All: *Jesus, You have found the lost,*
(sung)   *You have opened heav'n above;*
      You forgive us all our sins,
      You renew us with Your love.
      You have taught us how to care,
      You have giv'n us pow'r to live;
      We can look in all our needs,
      To the blessings that You give.

Tune: **Spanish chant or Martyn**

Midweek 2

As we gather, we spend a few moments in prayer asking the Lord to electrify our hearts as we experience His forgiveness and desire to share Jesus with others.

FATHER, FORGIVE
Lost Sheep

Luke 15:1-7

WE CELEBRATE

Lector: Welcome! Members of God's Family. We continue our Lenten celebration as we recall our baptism with the words that were spoken at our baptism.

Pastor: In the name of the Father and of the Son and of the Holy Spirit.

People: Amen

Lector: Come now to relive the first Word spoken from the cross:

Pastor: "Father, forgive them." (Luke 23:24 TEV)

Lector: And the Word spoken by Jesus in His parable of the Lost Sheep:

Pastor: "I am so happy I found my lost sheep. Let us celebrate." (Luke 15:6b TEV)

All: *Jesus, I will ponder now*
On Thy holy Passion;
With Thy Spirit me endow
For such meditation.
Grant that I in love and faith,
May the image cherish
Of Thy suff'ring, pain, and death
That I may not perish.

From *The Lutheran Hymnal,* © 1941
Concordia Publishing House

"Jesus, I Will Ponder Now"
Tune: **Jesu Kreuz . . .**

WE CONFESS

Lector: Let us confess our sins before God and in the presence of one another.

All: *Be merciful to me, O God,*
    because of Your constant love.
Because of Your great mercy
    wipe away my sins!
Wash away all my evil,
    and make me clean from my sin! . . .
I have sinned against You—
    only against You—
And done what You consider evil.

(Psalm 51:1-4a TEV)

All: *I, a sinner, come to Thee*
    With a penitent confession;
Savior, mercy show to me
Grant that all my sins remission.
Let these words my soul relieve:
Jesus sinners doth receive.

From The Lutheran Hymnal, © 1941
Concordia Publishing House

"Jesus Sinners Doth Receive"
Tune: Meinen Jesum

Pastor: "I tell you there will be more joy in heaven over one sinner who repents than over ninety-nine respectable people who do not need to repent."

(Luke 15:7 TEV)

To you who confess your sins, God gives His mercy and forgiveness.

WE CONVERSE

God Speaks

THE PARABLE OF THE LOST SHEEP

One day when many tax collectors and other outcasts came to listen to Jesus, the Pharisees and the teachers of the Law started grumbling, "This man welcomes outcasts and even eats with them!" So Jesus told them this parable:

"Suppose one of you has a hundred sheep and loses one of them—what does he do? He leaves the other ninety-nine sheep in the pasture and goes looking for the one that got lost until he finds it. When he finds it, he is so happy that he puts it on his shoulders and carries it back home. Then he calls his friends and neighbors together and says to them, 'I am so happy, I found my lost sheep. Let us celebrate!' In the same way, I tell you there will be more joy in heaven over one sinner who repents than over ninety-nine respectable people who do not need to repent."

(Luke 15:1-7 TEV)

We Speak

O Lord, may Evangelism be a happy time for us because we want to echo what goes on in heaven.

God Speaks

The Passion History according to
the Gospel of Saint Matthew
JESUS PRAYS IN GETHSEMANE
26:36-46

We Sing
"Jesus, in Thy Dying Woes"
Tune—**Septem Verba**

We Listen
The Homily

WE CONFIRM

With Our Offerings
(As our response to God's love and mercy)

With Our Prayers

Lector: We thank You, Father, that Jesus did as He told others to do, and forgave those who wronged Him.

People: Help us to forgive, no matter what the circumstances may be.

Lector: And so today we pray for those who do evil.

People: For blasphemers, unbelievers, heretics,

Lector: For those who exploit, tyrannize, and betray,

People: For the church where it denies the truth and ignores the evil,

Lector: For harsh leaders, unresponsive employers, and cruel parents.

All: Hear our prayer, O Lord.

Lector: We also pray for nations at war, that they may be led to peace;

People: For starving people, that others may share with them;
Lector: For oppressed people, that justice may prevail;

People: For families in bereavement, that they may be comforted.

All: Hear our prayer, O Lord.

Pastor: Into Your hands, O merciful God, we commend all for whom we pray, trusting in Your mercy, through Your Son, Jesus Christ, our Lord.

All: Amen.

WE COMMUNE

The Preface
The Distribution Hymn
"Christ the Life of All the Living"
Tune—**Jesu, meines Lebens Leben**

65

WE CONTINUE

Lector: As God has spoken to you this day,
He calls you to continue . . .

Pastor: To forgive your brothers as He forgives you,
To seek out the lost as He seeks those who are lost through you.
To rejoice over penitent sinners as heaven also rejoices.

People: *O Lord, help us to grow in our desire to speak words of forgiveness to one another, to reach out with words and deeds of witness to the unbelievers, and to demonstrate a spirit of great joy when people are baptized or confirmed or renewed in their faith.*

WE COMMIT

Lector: God now comes to you this day with His blessing:

Pastor: I will bless you and keep you,
I will make My face to shine upon you, and be gracious unto you,
I will left My countenance upon you and give you peace.

Lector: What is your response?

People: *We commit ourselves to His safekeeping,*
Mindful of sins forgiven,
Conscious of strength received,
Aware of peace restored.

Pastor: Go then, in peace. Serve the Lord.

People: *We shall. Amen.*

All: *Jesus, You have found the lost,*
(sung) *You have opened heav'n above;*
You forgive us all our sins,
You renew us with Your love.
You have taught us how to care,
You have giv'n us pow'r to live;
We can look in all our needs,
To the blessings that You give.

*Tune—***Spanish Chant or Martyn**

66

Midweek 3

As we gather, we spend a few moments in prayer asking the Lord for His goodness, grace, and generosity, so that we may trust Him and serve Him in His kingdom.

TODAY . . . IN PARADISE
Workers in the Vineyard

Matthew 20:1-16

WE CELEBRATE

Lector: Welcome! Fellow believers in God's kingdom. We continue our Lenten celebration with the greeting:

Pastor: The grace of our Lord Jesus Christ and the love of God the Father and the fellowship of the Holy Spirit be with you.

People: Amen

Lector: Come now to relive the second Word spoken from the cross:

Pastor: [The thief] said to Jesus, "Remember me, Jesus, when You come as King!" Jesus said to him, "I promise you that today you will be in Paradise with Me."

(Luke 23:42, 43 TEV)

Lector: And the Word spoken by Jesus in His parable of the Workers in the Vineyard:

Pastor: "So those who are last will be first, and those who are first will be last."
(Matthew 20:16 TEV)

All: *Sweet the moments rich in blessing*
Which before the cross we spend,
Life and health and peace possessing
From the sinners' dying Friend.

Lord, in loving contemplation
Fix our hearts and eyes on Thee
Till we taste Thy full salvation
And Thine unveiled glory see.

From *The Lutheran Hymnal,* © 1941
Concordia Publishing House

"Sweet the Moments Rich in Blessing"
*Tune—***Ringe Recht**

WE CONFESS

Lector: As we are assembled here to hear God's Word, and to call upon Him in prayer, let us first confess our sins before God and in the presence of one another.

All: Lord, as servants serving in Your kingdom, we find ourselves at times missing the joy of seeing Your goodness at work among us and around us and through us; failing to see Your grace operative in the lives of others because we are so concerned with a fair share of justice for ourselves;

neglecting Your generosity because of our petty jealousies and the fear that someone else is getting more than we have received.

Forgive us, O Lord, and fill our hearts with the knowledge of Your goodness, grace and generosity so that we may live useful lives in Your Kingdom.

Pastor: As Jesus, our Savior, received the penitent thief on the cross, so He receives you, forgives your sins, and offers His Spirit to you to help you be faithful Kingdom workers.

People: Amen.

All: In perfect love He dies;
  For me He dies for me.
O, all-atoning Sacrifice,
  I cling by faith to Thee.

Yet work O Lord, in me
  As Thou for me hast wrought;
And let my love the answer be.
  To grace Thy love has brought.

From *The Lutheran Hymnal,* © 1941
Concordia Publishing House
"O Perfect Life of Love"
*Tune—***Southwell**

WE CONVERSE

God Speaks

THE PARABLE OF THE WORKER IN THE VINEYARD
(Matthew 20:1-16)

We Speak

Lector: What, then, is your response to the Word of the Lord?

People: O Lord, thank You for calling us into Your kingdom; teach us to work and not ask for any reward save that of knowing that we do Your will.

God Speaks

The Passion History according to
The Gospel of Saint Matthew

THE ARREST OF JESUS
26:47-56

We Sing   "Jesus, Pitying the Sighs"
                                          *Tune—***Septem Verba**

We Listen   The Homily

WE CONFIRM

With Our Offerings

(As our response to God's grace and goodness)

With Our Prayers

Pastor: Let us speak to God confirming the faith that He gives us and the response that follows such a faith.

Lector: We adore You, O Lord.

People: For the gift of Your Gospel,
For the priceless gift of faith,
For the healing comfort of Your promises.

Lector: We confess, O Lord.

People: That You are our King,
Our Protector and Provider,
Our Savior and Redeemer.

Lector: We thank You, O Lord,

People: For the presence of Your kingdom,
For the workers in Your vineyard,
For the victory won by saints
called Home.

Lector: We ask You, O Lord,

People: To comfort the sick, the suffering, and the dying.
To inspire nations and people to seek peace.
To move us to be faithful workers in Your kingdom.

Pastor: Into Your hands, O merciful Father, we commit ourselves and all for whom we pray, trusting in Your mercy, through Your Son, Jesus Christ, our Lord.

WE COMMUNE

The Preface

The Distribution Hymn   "We Sing the Praise of Him Who Died"
                                   *Tune—***O Jesu Christ, mein's**

WE CONTINUE

Lector: As God has spoken to you this day, He calls you to continue:

Pastor: To make the love of God clear;
To explain the Gospel in an impelling way;
To invite people, in a winsome manner to respond to God who is good and gracious and generous.

People: *O Lord, help us to grow in our desire to speak Your Word boldly; to proclaim Your unmerited love to all who do not know You; to rejoice in being workers in Your kingdom.*

WE COMMIT

Lector: God now comes to You this day with His blessing.

Pastor: My peace which passes all human understanding, shall keep your hearts and minds in My knowledge and love; and My blessing shall be among you and remain with you always.

Lector: What is your response?

People: *We commit ourselves to God who called us to know Him, to receive His love; to experience salvation through Christ's death and resurrection, to enjoy the delight of His indwelling Spirit, to labor in His kingdom.*

Pastor: Go, then, rejoicing in His presence and serving in His vineyard.

All: *Jesus, You have found the lost,
You have opened heav'n above;
You forgive us all our sins,
You renew us with Your love.
You have taught us how to care,
You have giv'n us pow'r to live;
We can look in all our needs,
To the blessings that You give.*

Tune—**Spanish Chant** or **Martyn**

Midweek 4

As we gather, we spend a few moments in prayer asking the Lord to help us know Him better and experience His love more fully so that we might always minister to people with care, concern, and compassion.

BEHOLD . . . SON . . . MOTHER
Good Samaritan

Luke 10:29-37

WE CELEBRATE

Lector: Welcome! Sons and daughters of God. We begin our Lenten celebration hearing the invitation:

Pastor: I invite you to worship the true and living God
    the Father who made us
    the Son who redeems us
    the Holy Spirit who inspires us.

People: We shall, for we are His people, and we seek to worship Him in spirit and in truth.

Lector: Come now to relive the third Word spoken from the cross:

Pastor: Jesus saw His mother and the disciple He loved standing there; so He said to His mother, "He is your son." Then He said to the disciple, "She is your mother." (John 19:26-27 TEV)

Lector: And the Word spoken by Jesus in His parable of the Good Samaritan:

Pastor: "You go, then, and do the same," (Luke 10:37 TEV) that is, showing compassion to your neighbor.

All: *Lord of all nations, grant me grace*
    To love all men of every race,
And in each fellowman to see
    My brother, loved, redeemed by Thee.

    With Thine own love may I be filled
      And by Thy Holy Spirit willed,
    That all I touch, where'er I be,
      May be divinely touched by Thee.

From *The Lutheran Hymnal,* © 1941
Concordia Publishing House

"Lord of All Nations,
Grant Me Grace"
Tune—**Beatus vir**

WE CONFESS

Lector: One time, the apostle John wrote, "If we say that we have no sin, we deceive ourselves, and there is no truth in us. But if we confess our sins to God, He will keep His promise ...[and] will forgive us."(1 John 1:8-9 TEV) Therefore, let us make confession.

All: *We confess to being more concerned with others than those in our own family.*
We confess to being more concerned with who our neighbor is than being neighbor.
We confess to being more concerned with doctrine and traditions than with a personal involvement with people.
We confess to being more concerned with holiness and purity than down-to-earth love.

All: *Forgive me, Lord, where I have erred*
By loveless act and thoughtless word.
Make me to see the wrong I do
Will crucify my Lord anew.

Give me Thy courage, Lord, to speak
Whenever strong oppress the weak
Should I, myself, the victim be,
Help me forgive, remembering Thee.

From *The Lutheran Hymnal,* © 1941
Concordia Publishing House

"Lord of All Nations, Grant Me Grace"
Tune—**Beatus vir**

Pastor: You have the promise—the Lord forgives you.
You have the example—Jesus thought of others even when dying.
Go, and do the same. Amen.

WE CONVERSE

God Speaks

THE PARABLE OF THE GOOD SAMARITAN

"There was once a man who was going down from Jerusalem to Jericho when robbers attacked him, stripped him, and beat him up, leaving him half dead. It so happened that a priest was going down that road; but when he saw the man, he walked on by on the other side. In the same way a Levite also came there, went over and looked at the man, and then walked on by on the other side. But a Samaritan who was traveling that way came upon the man, and when he saw him, his heart was filled with pity. He went over to him, poured oil and wine on his wounds and bandaged them; then he put the man on his own animal and took him to an inn, where he took care of him. The next day he took out two silver coins and gave them to the innkeeper. 'Take care of him,' he told the innkeeper, 'and when I come back this way, I will pay you whatever else you spend on him.' " And Jesus concluded, "In your opionion, which of these three acted like a neighbor toward the man attacked by the robbers?" The teacher of the Law answered, "The one who was kind to him." Jesus replied, "You go, then, and do the same."

(Luke 10:30-37 TEV)

We Speak
>   *O Lord, help us to see that what we do for people in need, we do for You.*

God Speaks

The Passion History according to
the Gospel of Saint Matthew

JESUS BEFORE THE COUNCIL
26:57-75

We Sing

"Jesus, Loving to the End"
*Tune—***Septem Verba**

We Listen
The Homily

WE CONFIRM

With Our Offerings
(As our response to God's compassion and care)

With Our Prayers
Pastor: Let us pray for the whole people of God in Christ Jesus and for all persons according to their needs.

(Silence for individual prayer)

Lector: Almighty God, we pray for brothers, sisters, parents, children; for the sick, the troubled, the disturbed; for all those who are engaged in ministries of healing and service.

All: Show us how to reach out and help people You have left in our care.

Lector: We remember the lonely, the forsaken, the rejected, the homeless, the refugee, the forgotten; those in prisons, in institutions, in hospitals.

All: Help us to see You, O Lord, in every nameless neighbor.

Lector: We thank You for Jesus whose death showed the depth of His love and whose own concern for His mother demonstrated love in motion.

All: Direct us, O Lord, and move us to show compassion wherever and whenever possible.

Pastor: O Father, we ask You to hear our prayers and the prayers of all Your people, and fill our needs through Christ our Lord. Amen.

WE COMMUNE

The Preface

The Distribution Hymn

"O Perfect Life of Love"
Tune—**Southwell**

"Were You There?"
Tune—**Were You There**

WE CONTINUE

Lector: As God has spoken to you this day, He calls you to continue:

Pastor: To be a good neighbor;
To show compassion in a personal way;
To be a helper and healer for the helpless and hurting travelers along life's Jericho road.

People: O Lord, we belong to You. All that we are and have are gifts from You. We will pass through this way only once. Guide us to the people You have prepared for what we are to give in Your name.

WE COMMIT

Lector: God now comes to you this day with His blessing:

Pastor: I shall bless you as you come and go now and forever.

Lector: What is your response?

People: We go forth with His love in our hearts asking the question, "To whom can we show neighborly concern?" We go forth loving Christ first and then seeking to love our neighbor.

All: Jesus, You have found the lost,
You have opened heav'n above;
You forgive us all our sins,
You renew us with Your love.
You have taught us how to care,
You have giv'n us pow'r to live;
We can look in all our needs,
To the blessings that You give.

Tune—**Spanish Chant** or **Martyn**

Midweek 5

As we gather, we spend a few moments in prayer asking the Lord to fill our thirsty souls with the quenchable Water of Life.

I THIRST
Rich Man and Lazarus

Luke 16:19-31

WE CELEBRATE

Lector: Welcome! Followers of Jesus. We begin our Lenten celebration with the call:

Pastor: O come, let us worship and bow down, let us kneel before the Lord, our Maker.

People: He is our God; we are the people He cares for, the flock which He provides.

(Psalm 95:7 TEV)

Lector: Come now to relive the fourth Word spoken from the cross:

Pastor: Jesus knew that by now everything had been completed; and in order to make the Scripture come true, He said, "I am thirsty."

(John 19:28 TEV)

Lector: And the Word spoken by Jesus in His parable of the Rich Man and Lazarus.

Pastor: "If they will not listen to Moses and the prophets, they will not be convinced even if someone were to rise from death."

(Luke 16:31 TEV)

All: Chief of sinners though I be,
Jesus shed His blood for me;
Died that I might live on high,
Lived that I might never die.
As the branch is to the vine,
I am His, and He is mine.

O my Savior, help afford
By Thy Spirit and Thy Word!
When my wayward heart would stray
Keep me in the narrow way;
Grace in time of need supply
While I live and when I die.

From *The Lutheran Hymnal,* © 1941
Concordia Publishing House

"Chief of Sinners Though I Be"
*Tune—***Gethsemane**

WE CONFESS

Lector: It is time to open our hearts and minds to make confession.

Pastor: Almighty God, to whom all hearts are open, all desires known, and from whom no secrets are hid; cleanse the thoughts of our hearts by the inspiration of Your Holy Spirit, that we may perfectly love You and worthily magnify Your holy name, through Jesus Christ our Lord.

People: Amen.

Lector: We pause for a moment of silence for reflection and self-examination.

Pastor: Most merciful Father,

People: We confess that we are thirsty at times because we have all turned away from the only water that can satisfy our thirst, Jesus Christ, the Water of Life. When we try to go our own way, make decisions without You, and fail to listen to Your Word, we find ourselves in the desert where there is no water. Forgive us and help us always to cry out with the psalmist, "O God, You are my God . . . my soul is thirsty for You."
Amen. (Psalm 63:1 TEV)

All: I heard the voice of Jesus say,
"Behold, I freely give
The living waters; thirsty one,
Stoop down and drink and live."
I came to Jesus, and I drank
Of that life-giving stream.
My thirst was quenched, my soul revived,
And now I live in Him.

From *The Lutheran Hymnal,* © 1941
Concordia Publishing House

"I Heard the Voice of Jesus Say"
*Tune—***Vox dilecti**

WE CONVERSE

God Speaks
(Lector)

THE PARABLE OF THE RICH MAN AND LAZARUS

"There was once a rich man who dressed in the most expensive clothes and lived in great luxury every day. There was also a poor man named Lazarus, covered with sores, who used to be brought to the rich man's door, hoping to eat the bits of food that fell from the rich man's table. Even the dogs would come and lick his sores. The poor man died and was carried by the angels to sit beside Abraham at the feast in heaven. The rich man died and was buried, and in Hades, where he was in great pain, he looked up and saw Abraham, far away, with Lazarus at his side. So he called out, 'Father Abraham! Take pity on me, and send Lazarus to dip his finger in some water and cool off my tongue, because I am in great pain in this fire!' But Abraham said, 'Remember, my son, that in your lifetime you were given all the good things, while Lazarus got all the bad things. But now he is enjoying himself here, while you are in pain. Besides all that, there is a deep pit lying between us, so that those who want to cross over from here to you cannot do so, nor can anyone cross over to us from where you are.' The rich man said, 'Then I beg you, father Abraham, send Lazarus to my father's house, where I have five brothers. Let him go and warn them so that they, at least, will not come to this place of pain.' Abraham said, 'Your brothers have Moses and the prophets to warn them; your brothers should listen to what they say.' The rich man answered, 'That is not enough, father Abraham! But if someone were to rise from death and go to them, then they would turn from their sins.' But Abraham said, 'If they will not listen to Moses and the prophets, they will not be convinced even if someone were to rise from death.' "

(Luke 16:19-31 TEV)

We Speak
> *Lord, we hear Your message. To hear You, to believe in You, that means, we shall live—now and forever.*

God Speaks

The Passion History according to
the Gospel of Saint Matthew
JESUS BEFORE PILATE
27:1-31

We Sing

"Jesus, in Thy Thirst and Pain"
*Tune—***Septem Verba**

We Listen

The Homily

WE CONFIRM

With Our Offerings

(As one way to help a thirsty person)

With Our Prayers

Lector: Let us bring before God the needs of the church and the world.

(A brief silence for individual prayer)

Pastor: Father, You alone know all the needs of thirsty people. Help us to meet those needs in Your name.

77

People: *Give us sensitivity and compassion for all people. Help us minister to their needs whenever and wherever we can.*

Pastor: Into Your hands, O God, we commend all for whom we pray, trusting in Your mercy, through Your Son, Jesus Christ our Lord. Amen.

WE COMMUNE

The Preface

The Distribution Hymn   "Come, to Calvary's Holy Mountain"

*Tune—*Consolation

WE CONTINUE

Lector: As God has spoken to you this day, He calls you to continue:

Pastor: To thirst for Him;
To give a drink to the thirsty;
To listen to His Word;
To be ready and to be reassured of the greater life in heaven.

People: *O Lord, the basis of our eternal Hope is in our response to Your voice. You, the Author of life, have risen from the dead. That gives us new meaning for the present life and for the life to come. Help us to grow in our relationship with You today, tomorrow, and forever.*

WE COMMIT

Pastor: Go forth with the full assurance that God the Father, Son, and Holy Spirit, who has spoken to you this day, speaks each day to you to satisfy your needs.

People: *We shall, as we long for God's presence and share His gospel in words and acts and deeds with people.*

All: *Jesus, You have found the lost,*
You have opened heav'n above;
You forgive us all our sins,
You renew us with Your love.
You have taught us how to care,
You have giv'n us pow'r to live;
We can look in all our needs,
To the blessings that You give.

*Tune—*Spanish Chant *or* Martyn

Midweek 6

As we gather, we spend a few moments in prayer pouring out our hearts to God not afraid to voice our complaints. He understands. He is sympathetic. He is ready to listen and bring reassuring thoughts.

WHY FORSAKEN?
Widow and Judge

Luke 18:1-8

WE CELEBRATE

Lector: Welcome! Friends of Jesus. We begin our Lenten celebration with the greeting:

Pastor: We greet you in the name of the Father Almighty, the Son who suffered and died for you, and the Holy Spirit who speaks to you in His Holy Word.

People: *We have come to worship to experience spiritual blessings from our gracious God.*

Lector: Let us, then, celebrate as we relive the fifth Word spoken from the cross:

Pastor: "My God, My God, why have You forsaken Me?

(Matthew 27:46 NIV)

Lector: And the reason given by Jesus for His parable of the Widow and the Judge:

Pastor: To teach His disciples that they should always pray and never become discouraged.

(Luke 18:1 TEV)

All: *Throned upon the awefull tree,*
King of grief, I watch with Thee.
Darkness veils Thine anguished face;
None its lines of woe can trace
None can tell what pangs unknown
Hold Thee silent and alone.

Hark the cry that peals aloud
   Upward through the whelming cloud
Thou, the Father's only Son,
   Thou, His own anointed One,
   Thou dost ask him, Can it be:
   "Why hast Thou forsaken Me?"

Lord, should fear and anguish roll
   Darkly o'er my sinful soul,
Thou who once wast thus bereft
   That Thine own might ne'er be left,
Teach me by that bitter cry
   In the gloom to know Thee nigh.

From *The Lutheran Hymnal,* © 1941
Concordia Publishing House

"Throned upon the Awe-full Tree"
Tune—**Gethsemane**

WE CONFESS

Lector: Brothers and sisters in Christ, we are called to take off our masks before God, stand honestly before Him making confession and seeking forgiveness.

Pastor: O Father, we feel at times forsaken by You, but we must confess it is we who have forsaken You. When we do, we fear and fret, fumble and fail, and then blame You rather than face up to the fact that it is we who have forsaken You.

People: *Lord, have mercy upon us,*
Christ, have mercy upon us,
Lord, have mercy upon us. Amen.

All: *Chief of sinners though I be,*   *O my Savior, help afford*
   Jesus shed His blood for me;   *By Thy Spirit and Thy Word!*
Died that I might live on high,   *When my wayward heart would stray,*
   Lived that I might never die.   *Keep me in the narrow way;*
As the branch is to the vine,   *Grace in time of need supply*
   I am His, and He is mine.   *While I live and when I die.*

From *The Lutheran Hymnal,* © 1941
Concordia Publishing House

"Chief of Sinners, Though I Be" *Tune*—**Gethsemane**

WE CONVERSE

God Speaks

THE PARABLE OF THE WIDOW AND THE JUDGE

Then Jesus told His disciples a parable to teach them that they should always pray and never become discouraged. "In a certain town there was a judge who neither feared God nor respected man. And there was a widow in that same town who kept coming to him and pleading for her rights, saying, 'Help me against my opponent!' For along time the judge refused to act, but at last he said to himself, 'Even though I don't fear God or respect man, yet because of all the trouble this widow is giving me, I will see to it that she gets her rights. If I don't, she will keep on coming and finally wear me out!' " And the Lord continued, "Listen to what that corrupt judge said. Now, will God not judge in favor of His own people who cry to Him day and night for help? Will He be slow to help them? I tell you, He will judge in their favor and do it quickly. But will the Son of Man find faith on earth when He comes?"

(Luke 18:1-8 TEV)

We Speak
> *O Lord, we thank You for the encouragement You give us in the midst of our discouragement. Amen*

God Speaks

The Passion History according to
the Gospel of Saint Matthew
JESUS IS CRUCIFIED
27:32-44

We Sing

"Jesus Whelmed in Fears Unknown"
Tune—**Septem Verba**

We Listen The Homily

WE CONFIRM

With Our Offerings
> (As our response to God who does not forsake us)

With Our Prayers
Lector: I ask you to pray for God's people.

Pastor: Pray, brothers and sisters, for the church.

(Silence)

Lector: I ask you to pray for peace among nations; for goodwill among men; and for the well-being of all people.

Pastor: Pray, brothers and sisters, for justice and peace.

(Silence)

Lector: I ask you to pray for the poor, the sick, the hungry, the lonely, the oppressed, those in prison, those in mourning, those in distress.

Pastor: Pray, brothers and sisters, for all people in any need or trouble.

(Silence)

Lector: I ask you to pray for those seeking God and then desiring to grow in their faith.

Pastor: Pray, brothers and sisters, that they may experience God's presence and promises.

(Silence)

WE COMMUNE

The Preface
The Distribution Hymn   "When I Survey the Wondrous Cross"
Tune—**Hamburg**

WE CONTINUE

Lector: As God has spoken to you this day, He calls you to continue:

Pastor: To see Christ's suffering on your behalf,
To live in fellowship with Him;
To pray constantly, telling Him your deepest feelings.

People: *As we visualize the darkness at Calvary, hear the cries of the crowd, feel the pressures without and within, and hear again the cry, "My God, My God, why have You forsaken Me?" we know that we can continue to say, "God has not forsaken us!"*

WE COMMIT

Lector: We come to the close of our worship ready to go forth with the blessings of the Father, Son, and the Holy Spirit.

Pastor: Depart with the peace of God resting upon you.
Depart with the love of Christ dwelling within you.
Depart with the presence of the Holy Spirit abiding in your midst.

Lector: What is your response?

People: *We commit our lives to God who has given us His love, granted us His forgiveness, and renewed our spiritual lives.*

All: *Jesus, You have found the lost,*
You have opened heav'n above;
You forgive us all our sins,
You renew us with Your love.
You have taught us how to care,
You have giv'n us pow'r to live;
We can look in all our needs,
To the blessings that You give.

Tune—**Spanish Chant** or **Martyn**

Maundy Thursday

As we gather, we spend a few moments in prayer asking the Lord to help us sense His purpose for us in the victory cry, "It is Finished."

IT IS FINISHED
Wedding Feast

Matthew 22:1-14

WE CELEBRATE

Lector: Welcome, citizens of God's kingdom. We begin our Lenten celebration mindful of our baptism as we hear the words:

Pastor: In the name of the Father and of the Son and of the Holy Spirit.

People: Amen.

Lector: Come now to relive the sixth Word spoken from the cross:

Pastor: "It is finished." (John 19:30 TEV)

Lector: And the Word spoken by Jesus in His parable of the Wedding Feast:

Pastor: "My feast is ready now.
Come to the wedding feast." (Matthew 22:4 TEV)

All: *The Saviour calls; let ev'ry ear*
Attend the heavenly sound.
Ye doubting souls, dismiss your fear;
Hope smiles reviving round.

Dear Savior, draw reluctant hearts
To Thee let sinners fly
And take the bliss Thy love imparts
And drink and never die.

From *The Lutheran Hymnal,* © 1941
Concordia Publishing House

"The Savior Calls"
*Tune—***Azmon**

WE CONFESS

Lector: We now come to God, our Father, not because we must, but because we may, in order to confess our sins seeking His forgiveness through our Lord Jesus Christ.

All: *Father, we forget that we who have accepted Your invitation to the banquet feast have a call to grow in grace and mature in faith. Help us not to resist the change that You desire to bring about in us. Assist us to see that our faith is an on-going experience—sensing Your presence, seeking Your power, and searching Your purpose for daily living. Conscious of what Jesus has done for us, we cry out,*

All: *Lamb of God, pure and holy,*
    Who on the cross didst suffer,
Ever patient and lowly,
    Thyself to scorn didst offer.
All sins Thou borest for us, From *The Lutheran Hymnal,* © 1941
    Else had despair reigned o'er us Concordia Publishing House
Have mercy on us, O Jesus! O Jesus! "Lamb of God"

Tune—Christe, du Lamm

WE CONVERSE

God Speaks

THE PARABLE OF THE WEDDING FEAST

We Speak Matthew 22:1-14

Lector: What, then, is your response to the Word of the Lord?

People: *Help us, O Father, to clothe ourselves in the bright and shining "wedding garment" which Your grace provides for us through the life, death, and resurrection of Jesus Christ, our Lord.*

God Speaks

The Passion History according to
the Gospel of Saint Matthew

THE DEATH OF JESUS
27:45-56

We Sing "Jesus, All Our Ransom Paid"

Tune—Septem Verba

We Listen The Homily

WE CONFIRM

With Our Offering
    (As our response to the triumphal cry, "It is Finished")

With Our Prayers

Lector: Let us speak to God confirming our presence at His feast and our desire to have Him work constantly in us.

Pastor: We adore You, O Lord.

People: *For sins forgiven,*
For peace reestablished,
For salvation won.

Pastor: We confess, O Lord

People: *That Your accomplished work on the cross assures us that all things are*
ready at the banquet feast.

Pastor: We thank You, O Lord,

People: *For the gift of faith,*
For the joy of the present,
For the hope of tomorrow.

Pastor: We ask You, O Lord,

People: *To clothe us with Your righteousness,*
To enable us to work in Your kingdom,
To enjoy Your feast forever.

Pastor: Hear, O God, the prayers of our hearts

People: *In Jesus' name, we pray. Amen.*

WE COMMUNE

The Preface

The Distribution Hymn   "Go to Dark Gethsemane"
                                      *Tune—***Gethsemane**

WE CONTINUE

Lector: As God has spoken to you this day, He calls you to continue:

Pastor: To enjoy the marriage feast;
        To encounter God's presence each day;
        To invite others to come with you.

People: *Hearing Your call, O Father,*
        let us not only hear it, but do it;
        not only know it, but love it;
        not only believe it, but obey it.

WE COMMIT

Lector: God now comes to you this day with His blessing.

Pastor: Now may our Lord Jesus Christ Himself, and God our Father, who
        loved us and in His grace gave us unfailing courage and a firm hope,
        encourage you and strengthen you to always do and say what is good.
                                      (2 Thessalonians 2:16-17 TEV)

People: *We commit our bodies and our souls and all things to His direction.*

Pastor: Go in peace. Serve the Lord.

All: *Jesus, You have found the lost,*
You have opened heav'n above;
You forgive us all our sins,
You renew us with Your love.
You have taught us how to care,
You have giv'n us pow'r to live;
We can look in all our needs,
To the blessings that You give.

*Tune—*Spanish Chant *or* Martyn

Good Friday

As we gather, we spend a few moments in prayer asking the Lord to help us experience the new life that comes through His death.

IN THY HANDS
Mustard Seed

Matthew 13:31-32

WE CELEBRATE

Lector: Welcome! Brothers and sisters of the Lord. We begin our Lenten celebration hearing the voice of the apostle:

Pastor: Let us keep our eyes fixed on Jesus, on whom our faith depends from beginning to end. He did not give up because of the cross! On the contrary, because of the joy that was waiting for Him, He thought nothing of the disgrace of dying on the cross, and He is now seated at the right side of God's throne.

(Hebrews 12:2 TEV)

People: [Therefore] let us run with determination the race that lies before us.

(Hebrews 12:1a TEV)

Lector: Come now to relive the seventh Word spoken from the cross:

Pastor: "Father! In Your hands I place My Spirit!"

(Luke 23:46 TEV)

Lector: And the Word spoken by Jesus in the Parable of the Mustard Seed:

Pastor: The small mustard seed, that is planted, grows and becomes the biggest of plants, a tree.

(Matthew 13:31, 32 A paraphrase)

All: *Hark, how He groans while nature shakes*
And earth's strong pillars bend!
The temple's veil in sunder breaks,
The solid marbles rend.

'Tis done, the precious ransom's paid;
"Receive My soul!" He cries.
See where He bows His sacred head;
He bows His head and dies.

From *The Lutheran Hymnal,* © 1941
Concordia Publishing House

"Behold the Savior of Mankind"
Tune—**Windsor**

87

WE CONFESS

Lector: Christ died to set us free from the powers of darkness, death, and the devil. Let us confess our need of His freedom.

Pastor: From the darkness of sin caused by our rebellion against the law and love of God,

People: Good Lord, deliver us.

Pastor: From death with its sting as a result of our sins,

People: Good Lord, deliver us.

Pastor: From the devil—his empty promises, his demonic power, his evil presence,

People: Good Lord, deliver us.

Pastor: Christ is victorious over sin, death, the devil, and hell. He forgives our sins. He destroys death. He defeats the devil. Praise Him for the freedom He gives you.

People: Amen. All praise to You, Lord Jesus Christ.

All: *Lord Jesus, we give thanks to Thee*
That Thou has died to set us free;
Made righteous thro' Thy precious blood,
We now are reconciled to God.

Defend us, Lord from sin and shame
Help us by Thy Almighty name,
To bear our crosses patiently,
Consoled by Thy great agony.

From *The Lutheran Hymnal,* © 1941
Concordia Publishing House

"Lord Jesus, We Give Thanks to Thee"
Tune—**Old Hundredth**

WE CONVERSE

God Speaks

THE PARABLE OF THE MUSTARD SEED
Matthew 13:31-32

We Speak

All: *Lord Jesus, we hear You telling us that a seed dies before it springs forth into new life. When we die, with the name of Your Father on our lips and in our hearts, we are assured of a new life.*

The Passion History according to
the Gospel of Saint Matthew

THE BURIAL OF JESUS
27:57-66

We Sing

"Jesus, All Thy Labor Vast"
Tune—**Septem Verba**

We Listen   The Homily

WE CONFIRM

With Our Offerings
> (As our response to God's acceptance of us by means of Christ giving His life to God)

With Our Prayers

Lector: In our prayers, let us confirm the faith that is ours because of Christ's death on the cross.

Pastor: Heavenly Father, we thank You for Jesus Christ, especially for the words and actions that took place on the cross. Lord, in Your mercy,

People: Help us benefit from His example.

Pastor: Enable us to observe this day and the coming weekend with holy awe. Help us acknowledge the reality of our sins and the weakness of our faith. Lord, in Your mercy,

People: Lead us to the joy and power of the Resurrection.

Pastor: We pray for the sick, the sorrowful, the distressed, the dying, that they may be comforted. Lord, in Your mercy,

People: Hear our prayer of intercession.

> (Other Petitions and Thanksgivings may be offered)

Pastor: Into Your hands, O Lord, we commend all for whom we pray, trusting in Your mercy, through Your Son, Jesus Christ our Lord.

People: Amen.

WE COMMUNE

The Preface
The Distribution Hymn   "O Sacred Head, Now Wounded"

Tune—**Herzlich tut mich**

WE CONTINUE

Lector: As God has spoken to you this day, He calls you to continue:

Pastor: To grow in grace;
         To mature in love;
         To see death as a promotion to joy.

People: So we reflect upon the thoughts of Martin Luther in his explanation of the Seventh Petition of the Lord's Prayer and pray:
Our Heavenly Father, we pray that You would save us from every evil to body and soul and that at our last hour, You would mercifully take us from the troubles of this world to Yourself in heaven; through Jesus Christ, Your Son, our Lord. Amen.

WE COMMIT

Lector: God now comes to you this day with a blessing.

Pastor: God has raised form death our Lord Jesus, who is the Great Shepherd of the sheep as the result of His sacrificial death, by which the eternal covenant is sealed. May the God of peace provide you with every good thing you need in order to do His will, and may He, through Jesus Christ, do in [you] what pleases Him.
And to Christ be the glory forever and ever. Amen.

(Hebrews 13:20-21 TEV)

Lector: What is Your response?

People: *We commit all that we are and have to God with the assurance that He will strengthen our faith, keep us firm in His promises, and raise us up on the last day and give us and all believers in Christ eternal life.*

Pastor: Go forth in faith living with the Lord. Amen.

All: *Jesus, You have found the lost,*
You have opened heav'n above;
You forgive us all our sins,
You renew us with Your love.
You have taught us how to care,
You have giv'n us pow'r to live;
We can look in all our needs,
To the blessings that You give.

Tune—**Spanish Chant** or **Martyn**

Easter

Christ is risen! This is the feast of victory for our God. Christ steps forth from the grave alive. And we share in His resurrection, as we shared in His death.

"EASTER IS . . . PEACE"
Sower and Seed

John 20:19; Mark 4:3-8

PREPARING

As the Paschal Candle is brought into the sanctuary, the light of the candle symbolizes that the Light of Light, Jesus Christ, who appeared to be extinguished on Good Friday, is alive. This candle will burn for the next 40 days to remind us that Jesus was present visibly for 40 days before He ascended into heaven.

The choir enters singing:

> A suggested song for the choir is
> "He Is Risen! Alleluia!"
> —Michael Jothen/ Choristers Guild R-21

As the choir concludes the anthem, the congregation rises and turns to face the narthex. As the hymn is being sung, and as the Processional Cross passes, the congregation turns and faces the altar. The Processional Cross symbolizes Jesus Christ leading His people out of the world into His sanctuary.

> A suggested hymn for the congregation is:
> "Jesus Christ Is Ris'n Today"
> *Tune*—**Easter Hymn**

"EASTER IS . . . "

CONVERSING

Pastor: Good Morning! Easter is past! Why are you here?

People: It is the season of Eastertide, and we have come to celebrate the resurrection.

Pastor: The resurrection of our Lord, Jesus Christ?

People: Yes. And the resurrection of our own lives.

Pastor: How true! God raises Jesus Christ and also raises us to be His witness and heirs of eternal life.

People: *That's why we have gathered together to thank Him, to praise Him, and to respond to Him.*

Choir: This is the day which the Lord hath made.*

Pastor: This is the day which the Lord hath made.

People: *We will all rejoice and be glad in it.*

Choir: We will all rejoice and be glad in it.*

Pastor: He is Risen! Alleluia!

People: *He is Risen indeed! Alleluia!*

Choir: Alleluia. . . . *

* The choir responses are:
    "This Is the Day" —Jacobus Gallus/CPH 98-1702.
    • (This work is scored for double chorus. If choral forces are small, the second choral part may be performed by keyboard and/or instruments.)

CONFESSING

Pastor: We come together this day rejoicing in the knowledge of Christ's resurrection. Yet we acknowledge and confess we have often failed to live as resurrected people. Therefore, we make confession and ask for forgiveness.

(A brief silence)

Lector: O Lord, we confess that, like the disciples, we run away from Your death and try to hide from You.

All: *Forgive us, Lord.*

Lector: We confess our slowness to respond to the stone rolled back in our lives.

All: *Forgive us, Lord.*

Lector: We confess that the fear of death continues to haunt us in spite of Your victory.

All: *Forgive us, Lord.*

Pastor: Christ is risen. He is risen indeed! Today we stand forgiven before the empty tomb. We rejoice in that victory.

People: *Amen. Alleluia!*

"EASTER IS . . . "

A FACT   1 Corinthians 15:1-11

A SONG   Three stanzas with congregation and choir
             "I Know That My Redeemer Lives"
                                               *Tune—***Duke Street**

A MESSAGE	For the children
A RESPONSE	

Three stanzas with congregation and choir
"I Know that My Redeemer Lives"
Tune—**Duke Street**

ROLLING AWAY THE STONE	Mark 16:1-4
A SONG	An anthem by the choir
TELLING OUR JOY	**Matthew 28:5-8**

"EASTER IS . . . "

CONFESSING FAITH

Lector: Brothers and sisters, in what do you believe?

People: I believe in God, who created me.

Lector: And, what else?

People: I believe in Jesus Christ, who died to set me free and rose again to give me life.

Lector: And what else?

People: I believe in the Holy Spirit, the presence of God whom I experience in my life.

Lector: Anything else?

People: I believe that I, together with many others, belong to the family of God, people who have been resurrected to witness to His action and respond to His love.

Lector: And how do you do that?

People: I speak words of forgiveness, I do deeds of kindness and charity, I accept opportunities for service.

Lector: Let's, then, live our belief.

SINGING   "Awake, My Heart, with Gladness"
Tune—**Auf, auf, mein herz**

LISTENING	The Sermon
WELCOMING	Greeting the Worshipers
GIVING	Offerings

PRAYING

Lector: This is the feast of victory for our God!
Let us pray for the whole people of God, that they may share in this victory.

(A brief silence)

Lector: Let us pray that God will strengthen the church with newness of life.

Pastor: Sanctify Your church, O Lord.

People: That we may experience new life and faith.

Lector: Let us pray for all ministers of the church that they may faithfully share the good news of Easter.

Pastor: Clothe Your ministers with righteousness.

People: And let Your people sing for joy.

Lector: Let us pray for the nations of the world that peace and justice may prevail.

Pastor: Lord, keep peoples of all lands seeking peace.

People: And guide us to foster brotherly love and charity.

Lector: Let us pray for all who are in sickness or sorrow, especially . . . ; for all who are lonely or lifeless, fearful or frustrated, tempted or troubled.

Pastor: Let not the needy, O Lord, be forgotten.

People: Help us to share and serve whenever and wherever we can.

Lector: Finally, let us praise and thank our God for the feast of victory, which is ours through the resurrection of His Son, Jesus Christ.

Pastor: You are worthy, O Lord our God, to receive glory and honor and power.

People: You are worthy to receive blessing and praise, now and forever. Amen.

"EASTER IS . . . "

GETTING READY FOR HIS MEAL
Sing: "Hallelujah! Jesus Lives! *Tune*—**Fred til Bod**

THE WORDS OF INSTITUTION
Choir: Alleluia, Christ our Passover is sacrificed for us. Alleluia!*

Pastor: Our Lord Jesus Christ, the same night in which He was betrayed, took bread; and when He had given thanks, He broke it and gave it to His disciples, saying, "Take eat; this is My Body, which is given for you. This do in remembrance of Me."

Choir: Therefore, let us keep the feast with the unleavened bread of sincerity and truth. Alleluia!*

Pastor: After the same manner also He took the cup when He had supped, and when He had given thanks, He gave it to them, saying, "Drink ye all of it; this cup is the New Testament in My blood, which is shed for you for the remission of sins. This do, as oft as ye drink it, in remembrance of Me."

Choir: O Give thanks unto the Lord for He is gracious and His mercy endureth forever. Alleluia!*

*The Choir responses are:

"Christ the Passover"
—Healey Willan/CPH 97-4845

"EASTER IS . . . "

SHARING HIS PRESENCE
THE DISTRIBUTION HYMNS

The Distribution
"Christ the Lord Is Risen Today"
Tune—**Llanfair**

"Jesus Christ, My Sure Defense"
Tune—**Jesus, meine Zuversicht**

THANKING

A Prayer of Thanks

WITNESSING

Pastor: Go forth and tell everyone that Christ is risen!

People: We shall tell them that Jesus truimphed over death and the grave.

Pastor: Tell them that Christ is alive in the world today.

People: We will praise Him with our words and deeds. Alleluia!

RECEIVING THE BLESSING

SINGING

1. Now may He who from the dead
   Bro't the Shepherd of the sheep.
   Jesus Christ, our King and Head
   All our souls in safety keep!

2. May He teach us to fulfill
   What is pleasing in His sight,
   Perfect us in all His will
   And preserve us day and night.

3. To that dear Redeemer's praise,
   Who the cov'nant sealed with blood
   Let our hearts and voices raise
   Loud thanksgivings to our God.

From *The Lutheran Hymnal,* © 1941
Concordia Publishing House

"Now May He Who from the Dead"
Tune—**Orientis partibus**